TULIP

Reaktion's Botanical series is the first of its kind, integrating horticultural and botanical writing with a broader account of the cultural and social impact of trees, plants and flowers.

Tulip

Celia Fisher

REAKTION BOOKS

Published by
REAKTION BOOKS LTD
Unit 32, Waterside
44–48 Wharf Road
London N1 7UX, UK

www.reaktionbooks.co.uk

First published 2017

Printed and bound in China by 1010 Printing International Ltd

A catalogue record for this book is available from the British Library

ISBN 978 1 78023 759 6

Contents

Regions where wild tulips originate.

Red tulips.

one

Wild Tulips
ಜ್

O nce upon a time – as all the best stories begin – tulips grew unnamed and various in the valleys and slopes between distant mountain ranges. Their bulbs enabled them to endure ice-cold winters and fierce summer heat, in contrast to which the gentle sunshine and showers of springtime made them burst into flower. Their variations of colour, shape, size and other more intimate features must have been prompted by adaptations to their environment but seem also to be full of *joie de vivre*. When botanists seek out the origins of plants like this, so desirable that they have been widely distributed and hybridized, they arrive at the areas where the greatest diversity of wild species occurs. For tulips these areas are in the Tien Shan and Pamir-Alai mountains, which stretch for hundreds of kilometres across Central Asia in countries now defined as Uzbekistan, Kyrgyzstan and Tajikistan, and their remoteness feels like another element of the fairy story.

In these mountain passes, the ancient trading routes between China and the West, often known collectively as the Silk Road, were busy with merchants trading their plentiful wares, including livestock and plants, certainly fruit trees and probably tulips. Two tulip species, *Tulipa ferganica* and *Tulipa sogdiana*, carry ancient regional names. Fergana (see map) lay across the central area of the Silk Route where the Chinese came to buy horses with Arab blood which they described as 'bred from the wind'; Sogdiana bordered the Persian Empire in the west and produced the 'golden peaches of Samarkand', which to

Tulipa ferganica, in the Jangi Jol valley, Kyrgyzstan; it is also found in the Tien Shan and Pamir Alai mountains, and Fergana region of Uzbekistan.

Chinese poets were the food of the immortals.[1] The flowers of *T. ferganica* are buttercup yellow tinged with soft red/brown on the outside. *T. sogdiana* is smaller, with white flowers washed over with pale violet and a yellow centre. Like many wild tulips, both species can carry several flowers on one stem and they open out like little stars. Another tulip, bearing a more latter-day regional name, is *T. turkestanica*, which is related to *T. sogdiana* and has comparable colouring – ivory-white petals backed with duller purple and a large yellow centre; it is mainly distinguished by its nasty smell. Again it may have several flowers to a stem, much like *Tulipa biflora* itself – the tulip from which the whole, widely distributed, Biflora (also known as Biflores) group is named. In Western cultivation the best-known tulips of the Biflora group are *T. tarda*, originally collected from the northeastern end of the Silk Route among the Tien Shan mountains, and *T. polychroma*, which is native to Iran and Afghanistan and which is now considered to be a variant of *T. biflora* rather than a separate species.

This is a tiny foretaste of the diversity (not to say confusion) of tulip species which has arisen since the nineteenth century, when plant hunters started seriously exploring these regions. How do botanists distinguish whether a tulip is a separate species or simply a variant of the same species? The answer, as they would all admit, is with difficulty and disagreement. As A. I. Vvedensky, the authority on tulips of the USSR, wrote in 1935, 'the study of the genus *Tulipa* is beset with exceptionally great obstacles.'[2] Tulips love to naturalize, hybridize and even change their chromosome counts. Well over three hundred names of tulip species have been published, but the real number is probably fewer than eighty. On the other hand new species may still be discovered, like *T. cinnabarina*, a small, bright-red tulip from the Taurus Mountains of southern Turkey, described in the year 2000 and considered sufficiently different from others in its group (like *T. orphanidea* and *T. sylvestris*) to deserve its own specific name; or the red and yellow

Tulipa sogdiana, in the Kyzylkum Desert, near Khiva, Uzbekistan.

T. albanica – found in Albania in 2010 and related to *T. schrenkii*, one of the most widespread and colour-variable of tulip species.

To prove that this tulip story has all the elements of a treasure hunt, one of the tulips' main distinguishing features is hidden underground. The bulb of a tulip has a brown outer layer called the tunic, which may be tough and leathery or paper-thin and brittle. Inside the tunic there may be protective hairs, and the quantity of these suggests relationships. For instance, the species grouped round *T. clusiana* (including *T. montana* and *T. linifolia*) have a layer of hairs so thick that they stick out in tufts around the top of the bulb tunic. Early in the seventeenth century the herbalist John Parkinson noted

> this rare tulip wherewith we have been but lately acquainted … the root hereof is small, covered with a thick, hard, blackish shell or skin, with a yellowish woolliness both at the top and under the shell.[3]

One tulip, *T. lanata*, whose bright-red flowers adorn the rooftops of mosques in Kashmir, is named after the woolliness inside its bulb tunic. Other species, like *T. julia* and *T. agenensis*, have a matted layer like felt between the tunic and the bulb; some, like *T. fosteriana* and *T. eichleri*, have fewer, straighter hairs, giving a cobweb effect. Inside the tulip bulb, the energy for next year's growth is stored, and each year the plant must produce a new bulb. For good measure one or two little spares may grow at the base of the bulb – known as offsets, these are clones of the parent plant. In some species tiny new bulbs spread out on stolons (underground stems) away from the mature plant. Those that grow downwards, like *T. kaufmanniana*, are known as droppers (this is a protective device that tulip seedlings also favour). Other tulip species send their baby bulbs out horizontally, and if they reproduce this way rather than by seed they are known as stoloniferous – for instance, *T. clusiana*, *T. saxatilis*, *T. sylvestris* and *T. tarda* behave like this. To add to the variety of life, *T. hoogiana* (with red flowers that look almost black inside) forms little bulbils in the axils between its leaves and the stem.

The leaves of tulips grow alternately from the stem, sometimes in a rosette close to the ground, sometimes spaced up the stem. Typically they are long and thin, some more so than others, and generally grey/green. The surface may be either dull or shiny, and occasionally clear bright green, like *T. saxatilis*, and even more occasionally marked with dark dashes and stripes, like *T. greigii* and *T. eichleri*. One pale-yellow tulip that grows among the eastern ranges of the Tien Shan mountains in China is called *T. tetraphylla*, meaning four-leaved, but this indicates one over the odds rather than an exact number, because there may be up to seven leaves crowded at the base of its flower stem. Endearingly, some tulip leaves are wavy at the edges, especially when they have adapted to harsh environments, but this adaptive feature tends to be lost in easier conditions and in cultivation. As for tulip flowers, their wine-glass shape may range between oval and triangular, with rounded or pointed petals, flicking inwards or outwards at the tips. But the most basic contrast is between those with broad-petalled, bowl-shaped flowers – for instance *T. schrenkii* or *T. fosteriana* – and those with funnel-shaped flowers, an unromantic but correct term for the daintiest of tulips. It means they have narrow

Tulipa saxatilis, Royal Botanic Gardens, Kew. The first member of the Humilis group (also known as the Saxatiles) of tulips to be introduced to European botany early in the 17th century.

flowers with a slight constriction known as the waist between the base and the tips of the petals. The *saxatilis, sylvestris* and *biflora* tulips are like this.

To return to the question of hairiness, Eduard Regel, director of the St Petersburg Botanic Garden in the later nineteenth century, and a great name in the history of defining the genus *Tulipa*, divided tulips into two main groups according to the presence or absence of hairs on the filaments (the little stalks inside the flower which hold up the anthers covered in pollen). Despite attempts to create subdivisions, recent DNA and pollen studies have supported this overall classification. Plants in the Eriostemones group are fluffy around the filaments – this includes the Biflora group and those related to *T. saxatilis* and *T. sylvestris*. Those in the Leiostemones group have glabrous filaments (the botanic term for naked), including *T. clusiana, T. schrenkii* and *T. praestans*. While examining the inner parts of tulips it is also important to note that a tulip has six stamens (the male part of each plant, made up of filaments topped with pollen-producing anthers), varying among different species from golden to black. And the pollen colours differ too, being orange in the mauve-petalled *T. bakeri*, deep purple in the pink-and-white *T. clusiana*, and in *T. hageri* (first discovered on the slopes of Mount Parnassus) olive-coloured within a coppery flower. The female stigma and style (that receive pollen and enable it to reach the ovules, where seeds start their lives) generally form less of a feature in defining tulip species; it is only *T. orithyoides* (from Turkestan and in the Biflora group) that has a style so long it pokes out above the stamens and later develops into a beak on the ripe seed capsule, which is how it gets its name.

If the male and female parts are at the heart of the matter, it is still the appearance of the whole flower which attracts most attention, as nature intended when it created tulips to be fertilized by insects waking up in springtime. Normally a tulip has six petals, and there are no separate sepals surrounding the flower but there are distinct inner and outer layers of petals. Strictly speaking in such

cases the petals are called tepals, but this is one botanical term too
many. A feature that adds greatly to the charm of tulips is the variation between the inner and outer petals, which may be longer or
shorter; the outer petals are often narrower, with their backs stained
different colours. For instance the Biflora group has cream or white
flowers with the backs of the outer petals stained purplish or greenish grey; for *T. clusiana* and *kaufmanniana* the white or yellow outer petals
have red or purple backs; while *T. orphanidea* has burnt-orange petals,
the outer ones lightening to rich cream or deepening to green on
the reverse. Among garden tulips, the viridiflora have inherited from
a wild ancestor the green stripe that enlivens their pink, red, yellow,
orange or white petals. It is this propensity to colour variation that
has made tulips so widely collected and cultivated and has also led to

Tulipa turkestanica, a typical member of the Biflora group, in the Djbagly Reserve,
Kazakhstan.

Tulipa shrenkii (previously known as *T. suaveolens* or *T. odorante*, meaning sweet-smelling), from Pierre-Joseph Redouté's *Les Liliacées* (1805–16); showing the bicoloured characteristics the species sometimes has, even in the wild.

the proliferation of specific names – although petal colour is not the main guide in classification, because even a single colony of one tulip species can vary considerably in colour. In this it is *T. schrenkii*, from the Caucasus region, that takes the prize. One drift of this species can offer wine-red, pink, white and yellow forms, with the added bonus of a contrast colour edging the petals – a source of temptation so obvious that its westerly spread into cultivation and hybridization was inevitable. As the author of *Curtis's Botanical Magazine* wrote in 1805, alongside an illustration of *T. schrenkii*,

> we have been gratified with the sight of a large bed of this species of tulip, forming a carpet of scarlet and gold which, when illuminated by the sun, pour forth such a blaze of resplendent colouring as can hardly be conceived.[4]

Earlier, the species had been named as *T. suaveolens* from a cultivated form with a faint, sweet smell, and, although this feature is lost in its descendants, it is considered one of the main ancestors of modern garden tulips.

Inside the centre of a tulip flower more colour contrasts usually appear, known rather prosaically as the basal blotch, and this may be more indicative of a particular species than the overall petal colour. In both the creamy white Biflora group and the pink/magenta Saxatiles group the blotch is bright yellow and may cover most of the inside of the petals, adding greatly to the starry effect when they open. Even more dramatic are the black centres of many species of red tulip, either forming a circle, as in *T. agenensis* – which was formerly known as *T. oculis-solis* (eye of the sun) because the black blotch is often strikingly edged with yellow, like rays of light – or with the black blotch curving up to follow the shape of each petal, again enhanced by a rim of yellow, like *T. julia*, *T. eichleri*, *T. armena* or *T. lanata*. One variable species that caused particular confusion with its basal blotches was *T. humilis*, a small tulip related to *T. saxatilis*, with star-like flowers ranging from palest pink to crimson and magenta. Its basal blotch is usually yellow, but it may be blue, navy or purple and may be edged with white. To cover these contingencies *T. violacea* and *T. pulchella* were defined as separate species, but they are now regarded as variations of *T. humilis*. It was in this context that Anna Pavord was inspired to write 'tulips laugh at taxonomy';[5] and Daniel Hall, who produced *The Genus Tulipa* in 1940 (an authoritative but no longer definitive attempt to classify tulips), announced:

Tulipa pulchella, from
*Curtis's Botanical
Magazine* (1877),
a member of the
Humilis group
of tulips.

it is reasonable to regard this group as no more than a single
species, though in particular localities segregates have established which, by reason of their uniformity and power of
breeding reasonably true, may be worthy of subspecific rank.
The determination of a species must however always remain
a matter of opinion and judgement, into which the geographical distribution and the extent of variation in the field
should carry weight.[6]

Geographical distribution is, however, another conundrum. There
are groups of tulips, like the Humilis, Biflora and Sylvestris, in
which individual related species can be found all across Asia and

into Europe. Others appear to owe their travels to human intervention, while still others remain genuinely localized to definable areas. To begin in the eastern heartlands – the mountain ranges where the diversity of tulip species is greatest – the northern limits of tulip endurance lie among the Altai Mountains, which stretch from Mongolia into southern Siberia, northwestern China and northeastern Kazakhstan. Here the frozen winters are long and the short summers fiercely hot. The mountains give their name to *T. altaica*, whose flower is yellow with a red and green colour wash over its outer petals. Also growing here is *T. patens* (which is a relative of the widespread *T. sylvestris*), with white or palest-mauve flowers, the backs of the petals purplish green and the basal blotch yellow. But *T. patens* is not confined to the Altai Mountains; it grows westwards and is also to be found northeast of the Black Sea among the Caucasus mountains.

To the south of the Altai, the Tien Shan mountains stretch along the borders of Kyrgyzstan and Kazakhstan into the Chinese autonomous region of Xinjiang. About one-quarter of all tulip species are

Women in a Samarkand market, selling tulip bulbs gathered from the surrounding countryside, an age-old practice and one of the original ways that tulips were transported westwards.

Tulipa greigii, growing in the Tien Shan region of Kazakhstan, one of the major red tulips of Central Asia that has been brought into cultivation, and here also showing its capacity for colour variation.

concentrated here, including several of the Biflora (*T. turkestanica, T. tarda, T. bifloriformis* and *T. dasystemon*). Also to be found here are the dainty, predominantly yellow alpine tulips related to *T. altaica* – these include the extra-leaved *T. tetraphylla,* and *T. iliensis,* together with their bigger relatives *T. ostrowskiana* and *T. kolpakowskiana,* which have more red in their petals. In addition, there is the predominantly red-flowered group that includes *T. albertii* and *T. vvedenskyi.* But the best known are *T. greigii* and *T. kaufmanniana,* because they have been induced from their uplands home to flower in European gardens and add their genes to cultivated tulips. Both are capable of a wide variation of flower colour, and their tendency to hybridize when they grow together in the wild was noted by the collector John Hoog in 1902. He wrote to E. A. Bowles: 'the intermediate forms occur, but strange to say the influence of *T. greigii* only seems to come in the foliage.'[7] Certainly the characteristic leaves, with their striking purplish spots and dashes, add a garish panache to modern cultivars.

Southeast of the Tien Shan are the Pamir-Alai mountains bordering Uzbekistan and dominating Tajikistan, with the Himalayas to the east and the Hindu Kush mountains of Afghanistan to the south. Among the ranges nearest to Samarkand *T. fosteriana* is to be found, the largest of the Central Asian tulips with the broadest, glossiest leaves, tall sturdy stems and flamboyant red flowers. The petals are rounded and in the sun they open into a wide bowl, displaying black filaments and anthers set in a black blotch, boldly edged with yellow that zigzags round the base of the petals. This is the third in the triumvirate of showy wild tulips that have been bred for twentieth-century cultivars (of these, 'Red Emperor' is the best named) and also cross-bred with *T. greigii* and *T. kaufmanniana*. It is also an ancestor of the Darwin hybrids (see Chapter Eight). Another striking red tulip from this area is *T. praestans*, generously carrying several large flowers on a stem with petals that combine rounded and pointed characteristics as only tulips can. It is now well known in cultivation,

Tulipa kaufmanniana, the waterlily tulip, growing in the Djbagly Nature Reserve in Kazakhstan. It has become one of the most widely cultivated tulip species.

with a number of cultivars, but no hybrids. Some of the ubiquitous Biflora are also to be found in the Pamir-Alai, including *T. orithyoides*, with its beaky seed capsule.

Southeast again towards the Himalayas is the homeland of *T. clusiana*, one of the most widespread of wild tulips and among the first to arrive in Europe displaying the vivid colour contrasts that drove collectors to distraction. Usually *T. clusiana* is white with its three outer petals backed in deep-reddish pink edged with a pure white margin. Inside the flower there is another delicious contrast between the white petals and the deep-purple stamens in a purple blotch. Wherever it travels *T. clusiana* retains the deceptive frailty of an alpine plant and the slender elegance which has earned it the name 'Lady Tulip'. Its closest mountain relatives are *T. linifolia* from the Pamir-Alai and *T. montana* from the mountains of Iran; they all have extremely hairy bulb tunics, but the others lack the colour variability of *T. clusiana*. There is also a golden-yellow form of *T. clusiana* with terracotta outer petals edged in yellow. In the period when names proliferated this was considered a separate species, *T. chrysantha*, but it is now a variety, *T. clusiana* var. *chrysantha* (and there is a well-known cultivar called 'Cynthia'). Other variants from different areas, or with different features, were named as *T. stellata* (with a yellow blotch), *T. oreophila*, *T. chitralensis*, *T. grey-wilsonii* and *T. aitchisonii* – the latter has a dwarf habit and by far the most scientifically interesting claim to be a separate, or even the original, species. This is because, when the genes were counted, *T. aitchisonii* proved to be diploid, which is normal in wild tulips, meaning their chromosome number is $2n=24$. However, some wild tulips are triploid ($2n=36$), tetraploid ($2n=48$) and even pentaploid ($2n=60$). The larger gene counts, known as polyploidy, tend to make a tulip less fertile, and this is true of *T. clusiana*, which is pentaploid and stoloniferous (meaning it increases by sending out new bulbs on stolons rather than by seed). *T. clusiana* must have developed from an original, diploid, seed-bearing species, but this ancestral puzzle does not disqualify it from being the major tulip of its group. The natural distribution of *T. clusiana*,

The brilliant red *Tulipa montana*, Royal Botanic Gardens, Kew; native to mountainous regions of Central Asia from Turkmenia to Tabriz, and characterized by the hairy lining to its bulb tunic, a feature it shares with its relatives in the Clusiana group of tulips.

both white and yellow, may stretch as far west as Afghanistan and even Iran, where it can be found growing around Shiraz. Indeed, when it first arrived in Europe it was named *T. persica*. It is also one of the tulips found apparently wild in Turkey and southern Europe, but here it is believed to be a naturalized escape from cultivation.

Tulipa sylvestris offers a similar riddle of wild distribution and chromosome counts. The furthermost eastern reach of this group

Tulipa sylvestris, Royal Botanic Gardens, Kew. This gives its name to the Sylvestris group (or Australes) of wild tulips and has become naturalized across Central Asia and into Europe.

of tulips is represented by *T. patens* in the Altai Mountains, and they are also to be found high up in the Caucasus. But *T. sylvestris* is not an alpine species and its land of origin is unknown. It was first recorded growing in Italy in the sixteenth century but only around cultivated land, especially vineyards, and even as far east as Tabriz. Its discovery in 1927 was described thus: 'It occurs here mainly if not exclusively in orchards. It is sold in the streets in April towards the end of the month'[8] – both facts providing valuable clues that *T. sylvestris* was, many centuries ago, gathered in the wild for its appeal as a spring flower and spread happily (being stoloniferous) until it became a weed of cultivation. In Europe, naturalized colonies occur in France, Germany, Switzerland, the Netherlands, England, Sweden and even Norway, where it can be found near seaports. Since ships once carried soil as ballast, which at the end of the voyage might be dumped near the port, this is another clue to the journey of *T. sylvestris*. Possibly the English colonies were brought by the Romans with their vines, but if so they remained unrecorded for a long while. *T. sylvestris* is a tulip of golden charm, with a spicy scent and oriental pointed petals that curve back at the tips even in bud. The flower droops a little on its tall, swaying stem and the backs of the petals are darkly shadowed with grey/green. They open a little untidily and sometimes the petals number up to eight. This feature, together with their polyploid chromosome count (in Europe they are tetraploid) and their gypsy wanderings, have cast their wild status into doubt. It was argued that the smaller but very similar, yellow, *T. australis*, which is diploid and seeds more readily, and which inhabits the uplands of Mediterranean countries as well as Central Asia, behaves more like a truly wild flower and must be the ancestor of *T. sylvestris*. This whole tulip group is botanically known as the Australes, in deference to this possibility, but *T. sylvestris* retains its specific status, along with *T. primulina* from Algeria, which looks more fragile, being creamy white with purple/green shadows; and the ruddier *T. celsiana* from Morocco and southern Spain. Back in Asia, *T. sylvestris* has other close relatives besides *T. australis*. *T. bierbersteiniana* also has bright-yellow flowers shadowed with brownish green and could possibly be subsumed in *T. sylvestris* to help solve the question of the latter's wild origins. So could another lookalike, *T. urumiensis*, found near Lake Urumiya in Azerbaijan and northwest Iran. All these species are stoloniferous and willing to adapt to the kind of cultivation offered by orchards, meadows and vineyards.

The overall group of Australes also includes tulips of a reddish orange hue which have a dark basal blotch, unlike the yellow *sylvestris/australis* subgroup. Of these the leading species is *T. orphanidea*; native to the eastern Mediterranean including Greece, it grows particularly among pine trees, sharing the slightly windblown and decidedly oriental look of *T. sylvestris*. It too is variable in its gene count, sometimes diploid and sometimes tetraploid. One of its close relatives (some would say a subspecies) is *T. whittallii*, found in western Turkey (for instance around Izmir). The petals of *T. whittallii* are also pointed and curve backwards like the petals of *T. sylvestris* and *T. orphanidea*, but the flowers are rounder, neater and more beautifully coloured. They shine as temptingly as caramel, the outer petals brushed over the backs with cream. *T. hageri* is another coppery beauty with a green or buff wash on the backs of its petals and a striking olive-green basal blotch; again, this is native to the eastern Mediterranean and Greece (including Parnassus) and possibly it is simply a variant of *T. orphanidea*. As a further reminder of how specific names have been allowed to proliferate, *T. thracica* and *T. hellespontica* were named after the places of their discovery and separated from *T. orphanidea* because their stems and ovaries are hairier. *T. doerfleri* is not distinct for this reason, but because it is found in Crete; likewise *T. goulimyi* is distinguished because it is found in various Greek islands and has no basal blotch.

Among this hotchpotch *T. sprengeri* more clearly deserves its separate status, although it is another of the Australes group. It is a very upright plant with dainty, orange-red flowers rising among grassy leaves and petals so narrow at the base that gaps remain between them in the cup of the flower. The backs of the petals are suffused with olive green and there is no basal blotch, but the filaments interest botanists because they are not all the same length. *T. sprengeri* is found in the Pontic mountains of Turkey and flowers very late in the season, even waiting until June. The sequence of early, mid-season or late flowering has been used as another criterion for distinguishing different tulip species, and also cultivated tulips. In

English gardens *T. sprengeri* can be more readily induced to naturalize by seed than any other wild tulip.

To return to origins, although the Central Asian mountains remain the primary source, the Caucasus between the Black Sea and the Caspian are a second area where wild tulips are concentrated. And, in some cases at least, it seems to be from here that they spread, or were spread, westwards into Turkey and Europe. The colourful *T. schrenkii* mentioned earlier is the main example; another is *T. humilis*, the main representative of a group known as the Saxatiles (or Saxatilis group). *T. humilis* is a tiny low-growing tulip reminiscent of a crocus, with mauve/pink petals opening like a star and glowing inside with a yellow blotch and yellow stamens. But different locations of the Saxatiles group, and variations of botanical features and colour, especially the morphing of the basal blotch into purple and navy,

Tulipa shrenkii, flowering near Lake Korgalzhyn in Kazakhstan, showing the wide variation of colours that wild populations produce.

have all contributed to subdivisions: *T. aucheriana* and *T. violacea* from Iran; *T. kurdica*, which is redder; *T. pulchella* from Turkey; and *T. cretica* (which is white marked with pink), *T. bakeri* and *T. saxatilis* – all three from Crete, though *T. saxatilis* is also found in southwest Turkey. It was only because the last was the first to arrive into European cultivation in the seventeenth century that the group was named after it.

A showier tulip native to the Caucasus is *T. eichleri*, worthy to be linked with the large red tulips from further east like *T. fosteriana*. Its crimson-scarlet petals are slightly recurved, so that the flower has the shape of an inverted bell, and inside it the black basal blotch is edged with gold. Another fine red tulip from this region is *T. julia*, whose

Tulipa fosteriana, photographed in the Samarkand area of Uzbekistan; the largest of the glossy red tulips of Central Asia, here showing its dramatic black-and-gold basal blotch.

crimson cup has a greenish blotch, while the outside of the petal is washed either with white, giving the flower a pink blush, or yellow to tinge it orange. *T. julia* is also to be found in northern Iran and eastern Turkey, and a related group of tulips, of varying shades of red and occasionally yellow, inhabits different parts of the Middle East – *T. armena, T. aleppensis, T. praecox, T. systola* – and extends to the Balkans with the yellow *T. hungarica* and into northern Cyprus with *T. cypria*. This is yet another example of a tulip having been given the status of a separate species because it grows only in one particular region. But *T. cypria* has also been nicknamed 'the black tulip' because it is so deeply red, and perhaps also because the velvety richness of its colour, although in no sense black, summons the same yearning desire for a dark tulip that added to the frenzies of cultivators in seventeenth-century Holland, and indeed ever since.

Tulips can become an addiction and recent writers on tulips, however complex and botanical their descriptions of different species, have all borne witness to the thrill of finding a particular tulip growing wild. Anna Pavord began *The Tulip* with an amusing but lyrical description of searching for *T. bakeri* in Crete.[9] Diana Everett, as well as painting watercolours of wild tulips to adorn *The Genus Tulipa*, described the remote regions where she found them in flower – *T. regelii* for instance at Tamgaly-Tas, west of Almaty in Kazakhstan, where prehistoric folk have left carvings on the nearby boulders of hunting scenes and people dancing in a ring.[10] Richard Wilford, while untangling botanical complexities in *Tulips: Species and Hybrids for the Gardener*, wrote: 'if you are lucky enough to find yourself in this situation it may be better to give up on the names and just enjoy the tulips for what they are.'[11]

Painting of the three sons of Shah Jahan, with borders of tulips and flowering plants, *c.* 1635, watercolour and gold on paper.

two

Turkish Tulips
🪶

The collection, cultivation and artistic representation of tulips all began in the East, but beyond the certainty of that statement a tantalizing obscurity sets in. The Turks deserve most but not all of the credit for realizing the potential of tulips, because Persian poets and Mughal emperors were also fond of them. The Afghan warlord Babur, who founded the Mughal dynasty of India early in the sixteenth century, created palaces and much-loved gardens in the cities that he conquered and ordered that tulips should be planted in them. Presumably they were collected in the wild, and he himself recorded 33 different kinds in the plains of Kabul; when he later reached Samarkand he made sure to visit the tulip meadows there. Babur's great-grandson Jahangir also created gardens on an extravagant scale, but his favourite was in Kashmir: 'in the soul enchanting spring', he wrote in 1620, 'the hills and plains are filled with blossoms, the gates, the walls, the courts, the roofs are lighted up by the torches of tulips.'[1] His court artist Ustad Mansur painted an album of Jahangir's favourite flowers, including a tulip whose scarlet petals sing out. It is probably *T. lanata* (the highland tulip named after the woolly lining of its bulb tunic), which had been introduced into Kashmir from the Pamir-Alai and was often planted on the roofs of mosques, possibly for some religious or protective association.

There is an oriental legend about red tulips which derives from the prehistory of mankind, when the revival of nature in springtime was at the heart of urgent and possibly bloodthirsty rituals, and red flowers blossoming across the cold, bare earth were a potent signal of rebirth. They represented the blood of Farhad, who loved the unattainable princess Shirin. In the Persian version retold by the twelfth-century poet Nizami, she was married to Shah Khosrow, who had searched for her backwards and forwards across Asia (one favourite miniature illustrating the story showed him watching her bathing, neither knowing who the other was). Alternatively, in the fourteenth-century poem by Hafiz, she was already married to Khosrow and it was Farhad who wandered through the wilderness calling her name. But both poets then tell how Khosrow challenged the persistence of Farhad's love by setting a challenge. If Farhad could cut through rock and cause a stream to flow through to the other side of the mountain, Shirin would be relinquished to him. Farhad had almost accomplished his task when Khosrow sent him the false message that Shirin was dead. In despair Farhad threw himself from the top of the mountain, and among the blood-drenched rocks in the valley below, tulips sprang up. This tragic love appealed to poets, as this quatrain by Hafiz shows:

> And where the tulip following close behind
> The feet of spring, the scarlet chalice rears
> There Farhad for the love of Shirin pined
> Dyeing the desert red with his heart's tears.[2]

In the Turkish version of the story the mountain is named after the hero, and it was Shirin's father who commanded him to tunnel through the rocks to bring spring water to his palace, and who sent the cruel, false message when Farhad was on the point of success.

Storytellers are time-honoured figures, plying their trade all across Asia, and naturally the legend was adjusted for different epochs and tribes, and then again by court poets, until the element of ritual sacrifice was almost suppressed. But the traces remain of the lost girl, like Persephone or Eurydice, the search through the wilderness, the impossible challenge, and the bringing of water and fertility. There

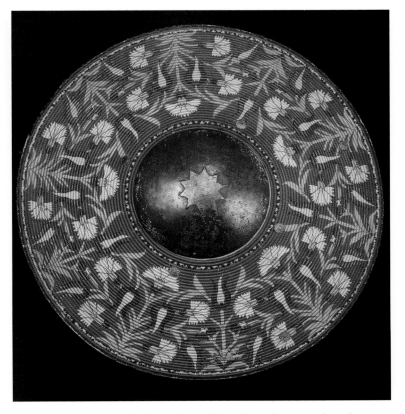

Ottoman wicker shield with a steel central boss, late 16th century; the wicker is decorated with alternating tulips and carnations in silk and gold threads.

are many similar echoes (though without tulips) in Greek, Arthurian and Nordic legend and in the Indian story of Rama and Sita. And other red flowers are linked with heroic blood – anemones with Adonis, who fatefully loved Venus, and poppies with battlefields. So although tulips do not have traditional symbolism in Europe, they do in their heartlands.

For the Turks, as they made their way westwards, tulips also became a powerful talisman. They decorated many items connected with travel and war – prayer rugs, tents, water bottles, arms, armour, boots and even the saddles of horses. Circular Turkish shields formed from wicker (woven like basketry around a metal centre) were lined with silk bearing symbolic motifs including tulips. In 1389 at the battle of Kosovo the Ottomans defeated the Serbs, although it was a massacre on both sides, and the chronicler described the battlefield strewn with the dead still wearing their colourful turbans like a gigantic bed of tulips.[3] The victorious Prince Bayezid, nicknamed 'The Thunderbolt', survived to become Sultan Bayezid I. In battle he wore a surcoat embroidered with verses from the Koran on the front and tulips on the back, and during the following decade his armies advanced through Bulgaria and northern Greece. But his luck ran out in the East when Tamburlaine attacked Anatolia and he was captured at the battle of Ankara in 1402, an event cataclysmic enough to be recorded in England and dramatized by Christopher Marlowe. The Persian poet Hafiz, although he died around 1390 and knew nothing of this event, certainly knew of Tamburlaine's conquests and of life's uncertainties. (According to one tale Hafiz was summoned to court to explain a love poem in which he vowed he would exchange Samarkand and Bokhara – Tamburlaine's finest cities – for his lady's black mole.)

> Perhaps the tulip knows the fickleness
> Of Fortune's smile, for on her stalk's green shaft
> She bears a wine cup through the wilderness.[4]

The link between tulips and wine glasses was irresistibly apt and had been formulated by Omar Khayyam two centuries before:

> As then the tulip for her morning sup,
> Of heavenly vintage from the soil looks up
> Do you devoutly do the like, till heaven
> To earth invert you, like an empty cup.[5]

Whether one believes that the Persian poets were extolling drunken oblivion or, like true Sufis, using it as an analogy for mystic union with the divine, they certainly provided a rich vein of inspiration

Tile created by the Seljuk Turks, who occupied Anatolia in the 12th century and were the first to decorate ceramics with tulip designs.

for later Turkish versifying. In 1453, when Sultan Mehmet II, 'the Conqueror', finally captured Constantinople, it had become a ghostly remnant of the old Byzantine Empire, although its walls were strong. Mehmet rebuilt it as Istanbul, a wonderful place with mosques, palaces, fountains and gardens full of tulips, the greatest of which was Topkapi Saray. The Conqueror also wrote couplets: 'Pour more wine cupbearer, for one day / The tulip garden will be destroyed.'[6]

Were the tulips in Mehmet's gardens already cultivars or were they gathered in the wild? Turkey certainly has wild tulips; there are fourteen species listed in the *Flora of Turkey*, most notably *T. armena*, which has rounded flowers in variable shades of red and yellow, and the very similar *T. julia*, distinguished mainly by the thick, felted lining of its bulb tunic.[7] These two species are far more likely to have contributed their genes to garden tulips than another two genuinely indigenous tulips, *T. biflora* and *T. humilis* (or any rare and recent discovery like *T. cinnabarina*). There are also tulips now growing wild in Turkey, but naturalized in cultivated ground, so they were probably introduced from further east (whence they have spread across the Middle East and even into Europe); these include *T. clusiana, T. agenensis* and *T. praecox*. The last looks more like a garden tulip than most wild species do: it has a thick stem and outer petals that are longer and more pointed than the rounded inner petals, it is orange-red with green streaks on the outer petals and yellow on the inner ones. The Turks surely contributed to the westwards spread of these species. The Seljuk Turks, from whom the Ottoman Turks were descended, settled in eastern Anatolia and expressed their appreciation of tulips as early as the twelfth century by including them in the designs of ceramic tiles, with which they adorned the mosques and palaces of Konya. As the Ottoman Turks pressed further with their conquests there were more wild tulips to discover, including the wonderfully variable and adaptable *T. schrenkii*. Its petals form a shape reminiscent of the idealized tulip of sixteenth-century Turkey, rounded at the base and pointed at the tips. It is to be found in Central Asia, the Caucasus and the Russian steppes, but the Turks probably discovered *T. schrenkii* after they annexed the Crimea in 1475, since it reached the flower markets of Istanbul under the name of *kefe lale*. Kefe was the province in the Crimea (now Feodosiya) where Suleyman the Magnificent was governor before he became sultan in 1520. *Lale* was the Turkish, and Persian, name for tulip and, because the same calligraphic characters formed the word Allah, this added a religious dimension to the flower's cultural significance. The word *lale* was also a gift to Turkish poets because it rhymed with *piyale*, a wine glass.

It was from this rich mix of tulip species – which had no opportunity to hybridize in their separate wild habitats before they were collected into Turkish gardens – that cultivated tulips first evolved, although the Turks gave no hint that they expedited the matter but simply said that they 'occurred'. As proof of tulips' importance, and perhaps also of their increasing variety, the reign of Suleyman the Magnificent (1520–66) saw an explosion of them in many forms of art as well as on the Sultan's own robes, battle helmet and armour. Luxurious silks, embroideries, velvets and brocades were not new,

Section of a kaftan
with tulip markings,
said to have belonged
to Suleyman the
Magnificent,
mid-16th century.

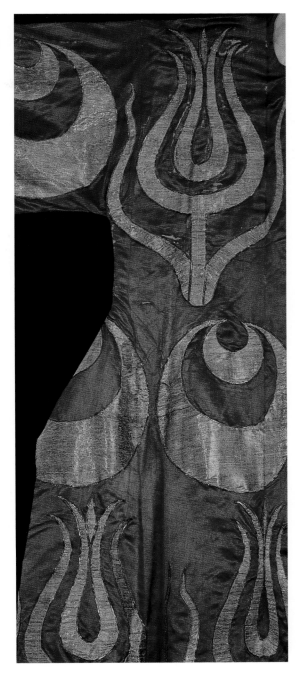

A tulip on an İznik tile in the 16th-century mosque of Rustem Pasha, Istanbul.
The patterns on the tulip petals are a fanciful representation of the flower's colour
variations, and the contrasting area of the basal blotch is also suggested.

but they reached new heights of production, both as furnishings to spread across beds and divans, and for clothing. One such garment was the kaftan, which was a long, wide-sleeved and adaptable garment; it could be lined with fur for winter warmth and up to three could be worn in layers, as described in 1533 by the Venetian emissary Marino Sanuto:

> the commander [of the Ottoman fleet] is a youngish man of about 38 with reddish moustaches and a handsome appearance. He wore a turban of the finest cloth and was seated cross-legged in the Turkish manner. Over his shirt he wore a gown of yellow satin, and over that one of damask with great flowers in gold thread. Over that he had one in scarlet.[8]

How one would like to know whether those 'great flowers' were tulips; maybe the Venetian did not name them because he had never seen a tulip. Other flower and fruit motifs on sixteenth-century Turkish fabrics included the stylized lotus derived originally from China, pomegranates, carnations, roses and fruit blossom, but tulips were the most distinctive, and whether large or small they were always formed of three curving petals. Turkish ceramics outdid textiles in the widespread use of this same stylized tulip motif, although being predominantly blue they were even less reliable as a botanical record (blue is a colour tulips rarely achieve, and then only in their basal blotches). Another quirk often seen in the tulips featured in ceramics is a contrasting colour at the base of the petals shaped like sepals, which tulips do not have. These represent basal blotches, which the Turks obviously felt should be included even though they are not usually visible on the outside of the flower, and perhaps the spots and stripes on the petals of such ceramic tulips suggest their appreciation of bicoloured forms.

The earliest reference to the production of İznik blue-and-white ware, in emulation of Ming porcelain from China, survives in the kitchen accounts of Sultan Mehmet II from around 1470.[9] The first

İznik plate showing a red tulip with blue spots, late 16th century. The red of the glaze and of the tulip were both highly prized; the blue spots were artistic licence.

colour to be mastered was cobalt blue and the early patterns had a strong chinoiserie element. Tulips entered the repertoire midway through the reign of Suleyman, around 1535, as did the turquoise glaze. Soon after came sage green, and around 1560 the rich and highly prized red, the colour that could do justice to the reality of tulips. This was created from a bright-red earthy clay called Armenian bole, making a glaze so tricky that it caused much wastage of defective pieces and led eventually to the decline of the İznik potteries. This brief blaze of colourful, tulip-laden glory could be seen not only on dishes, bowls and jars but on the tiles that decorated the most stunning buildings of sixteenth-century Istanbul. These included Suleyman's own mosque, the Suleymaniye, commanding the skyline

Turkish fabric with tulip embellishments, a detail from a kaftan probably worn during the reign of Selim II, who succeeded Suleyman the Magnificent in 1566.

of the city seen from the water and designed by Sinan, the famous court architect of the age. Other mosques designed by Sinan were endowed by the grand viziers Rustem Pasha (who married Suleyman's daughter Mihrimah Sultan in 1539) and later Sokollu Mehmed Pasha, vizier to Selim II. Both these mosques had to be cunningly fitted into

View of Suleymaniye, showing blossom trees and tulips, from an account
of the campaigns of Suleyman the Magnificent during 1534–5, in the
16th-century manuscript *Mecmua-i Menazil*.

smaller urban spaces than the Sultan himself commanded, but both had tilework even more varied and exquisite. The mosque of Rustem Pasha was built on a high terrace over vaulted shops near the spice market and was reached by narrow, twisting stairs which open suddenly into a wide courtyard. Tiles cover every wall: the facade, the fountain, the interior, the mihrab and the columns. No other mosque makes such lavish use of tiles with such imaginative tulip designs; however, a slightly later mosque, built beside the Hippodrome in the centre of Istanbul by Sultan Ahmed I between 1609 and 1616, and known affectionately as the Blue Mosque, boasts thousands of Iznik tiles and fifty different tulip designs – but many of these are so high up that their details are lost in the grandeur of the space. The Topkapi Palace, the great treasure house of Istanbul, is an indoor garden maze, where corridors and courtyards offer a feast of tulip tiles in an atmosphere charged with mystery. The palace was first built by Mehmet the Conqueror in the fifteenth century, but its present appearance owes more to Suleyman's grandson Sultan Murad III, who restored the palace around 1574, when he succeeded Selim II. Suleyman's descendants spent more time inside the palace than Suleyman himself, since they abandoned the energetic practice of leading military campaigns themselves. Within its spacious grounds sloping down to the Bosphorus, the palace was designed around four great courtyards, each more secret than the last. The fourth was where the tulips grew.

Another luxury to which the Ottoman sultans devoted their patronage was the production of illuminated manuscripts, including Korans in which the flowers of paradise were scattered over pages sheeted in blue and gold. The skills of the calligraphers and illuminators were developed in the imperial chancery, copying edicts, judgements, treaties and accounts, which were authenticated by the *tughra* – a huge calligraphic signature – of the sultan, and here too tiny flowers including tulips started to appear during the 1550s. But the most singular manuscripts of Suleyman's reign were the dynastic histories which concentrated proudly on Ottoman conquests,

Lacquer binding of a book, decorated with garden flowers including tulips, created for prince Sehzade Mehmet (d. 1543), son of Suleyman the Magnificent.

with views of the cities through which the Turkish armies passed. In *Mecmua-i Menazil*, which detailed Suleyman's eastern campaign against Shah Tahmasp I of Persia during 1533−5, there is a view of Sultaniye in northwestern Iran, where the green countryside around the city blossoms with fruit trees and flowers including red tulips. Only the breached walls of the city indicate that this was a war zone; otherwise all is delight, with wandering streams, pink palaces, pavilions, mosques and shrines, deer and scampering rabbits − a perfect setting for tulips that are wild and covetable.

A more cultivated garden setting is suggested in the binding of a book of religious texts and prayers (*hadith*) made for Suleyman's son Sehzade Mehmet, who died in 1543. (Since he was the intended heir, the oldest son of Suleyman's beloved wife Hurrem Sultan, his death precipitated conspiracies and executions.) The binding is lacquered

Detail of a manuscript illumination showing tulips, from the *Divan-i Muhibbi* (1566),
a collection of poems written by Sultan Suleyman.

and set with naturalistic flowers – a yellow rose bush in the centre,
fruit blossom, dianthus, violets and an iris, and tulips sporting their
colours, red and blue, but more interestingly several seem to be bicoloured in a naturalistic way. Such comparative naturalism was new,
and seen as a feature that developed during Suleyman's reign as a
direct result of the increasing use of floral motifs in various art forms.
The strong contrast of genres between fantastic patterning and the
true form of a much-loved flower can be seen in the pages of the
Divan-i Muhibbi. This was a collection of Suleyman's own poems, his
divan, and Muhibbi was his pen name, meaning 'the affectionate one'.
It was illuminated by Kara Memi, the leading court artist, and signed
off in 1566, the year Suleyman died. Kara Memi was innovating when
he created these little flowerbeds as vignettes between the lines of
verse, in strong contrast to the chintzy borders. The poems were
mainly gazelles (comparable to sonnets) using the traditional Persian
vocabulary of nightingales and roses, and faces as fair as tulips. But it
still comes as a surprise that the battle-hardened father of the nation,
the lawgiver, scourge of his neighbours, bogeyman of Europe, known
at home as the keeper of men's necks, could write so languorously of
pleasure:

> Come and drink muscat wine in the garden
> Do not believe that drunkenness is shameful

Nor is it against the law
A Frankish slave has poured the wine
Muhibbi do not let the occasion pass
Nor let your hand stray from the tulip-red wine.[10]

Tulips were not just for sultans. Foreign visitors exclaimed at how the populace loved flowers, hawking them in the streets and markets. The French botanist Pierre Belon, who visited Turkey in 1546–9, was the first to describe there a 'red lily' unlike any he had seen in Europe. He wrote admiringly of Turkish gardens and how 'no people delight more to ornament themselves with beautiful flowers, nor praise them more than the Turks.'[11] Another Frenchman, Fresne Canaye, who was in Istanbul in 1573, wrote: 'they always carry a tulip in their hand or set in their turban.'[12] Turkish miniatures sometimes testify to this habit, as do tombstones headed by a carved turban with tulips tucked into the folds (these were for citizens, not sultans, the latter of whom would wear massive jewels in their turbans). The Austrian ambassador to the Ottoman Empire, Osias Busbecq, who has been credited with introducing tulips into Europe, is also associated with their naming. The Turkish for tulip is *lale*, while the name 'tulip' and its variants in other European languages derived from *tulban*, the Turkish for turban. Presumably Busbecq pointed to the flower to ask its name and was mistakenly given the word for the headgear. Even if the story is wrongly attached to Busbecq, the etymology of 'tulip' seems unavoidably linked to some such misunderstanding.

Since the reign of Mehmet the Conqueror (1451–81) records exist of garden flowers being sold in the markets of Istanbul, but many more tulips at this time were still being brought in from the wild. 'You cannot stir abroad', wrote George Sandys early in the seventeenth century, 'but you shall be presented by the dervishes and janissaries with tulips and trifles.'[13] It seems odd that his exasperation was directed at these particular representatives of the religious and military community, who would have been unlikely to stoop to street trading. But another English traveller, Peter Mundy, an employee of

Bedsheet embroidered with tulips, created in Istanbul in the second half of the 16th century.

the East India Company, who was in Turkey from 1617 to 1620, made a more charming link between a janissary and tulips when he created a scrapbook.[14] This consisted of cut-outs of flowers and Turkish characters in costume which, like the tulips themselves, Mundy would have found in the local markets. Mundy's cut-out tulips, though

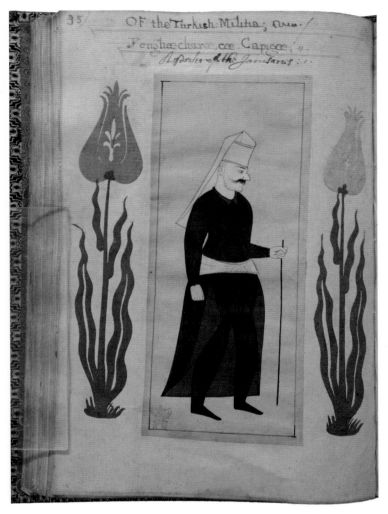

Cut-out paper decorations in the form of tulips, surrounding a portrait of a janissary, from *A Briefe relation of the Turckes*, a scrapbook created by the English traveller Peter Mundy (1618).

stylized, retain the sturdiness of wild flowers and have wavy edges to their leaves. The seventeenth-century Ottoman travel writer Evliya Celebi made it clear that wild tulips were a familiar sight to the citizens of Istanbul, when he described picnicking in the meadows of Kagithane:

Float with a large yellow tulip, decorated for the wedding of Ibrahim Pasha in 1524, watched by the Sultan, from *Surname-i Humayun* (The Imperial Book of Festivals, 1582–3).

A delightful river flows through the valley to the Bosphorus . . . on both sides are meadows with clover, ranunculus and tulips and shady bowers with plane trees and willows. On holidays thousands come to flirt and boat and swim with musical entertainments in every corner; and guild festivals are held with pavilions and parties.[15]

Turkish manuscripts illustrate the greatest festivals of all, held by the sultans to celebrate weddings and circumcisions, and flowers were a feature of the processions. In 1582 Murad III's celebrations for the circumcision of his son lasted 52 days. In the Hippodrome there were mock sieges and battles, acrobats and buffoons, firework displays and so many flowers that they scented the air. Among the floats (some of which, the *sukker nakkaslan*, were made from candy and marzipan) miniature gardens and towering tulips were represented. In illustrations of these festivals the developing shape of the Ottoman tulip can be seen, and it was probably not until the eighteenth century that the fantastically elongated 'needle' petals were fully achieved. There is one wild tulip, *T. acuminata*, which would seem an obvious ancestor. Its pointed petals are creamy yellow streaked with red – thin, long and slightly twisted, as if it were under a spell. In a sense it is, because this is not a genuine wild species, although it has been given a specific name; it is an escape from cultivation and presumably a survivor of that extraordinary era in Turkey from which no cultivar remains. *T. acuminata* arrived in Europe in 1811 and was illustrated in Pierre Joseph Redouté's *Les Liliacées*, dedicated to Empress Josephine, in 1815. But it remains a mystery how those skeins of colour were originally induced to breed, and from which ancestral tulips collected in Ottoman plant nurseries.

Tulipa acuminata, (then known as *Tulipa cornuta*) from Pierre-Joseph Redouté's *Les Liliacées* (1805–16).

Sultan Selim II (1566–74) was crazier about tulips than his father Suleyman; in fact he was nicknamed 'The Sot' and a kiosk painted with tulips was built for him to while away his time beside the Bosphorus. His provincial governors were ordered to send him thousands of wild tulips and specialist nurserymen bred cultivars, the first on record being Seyhulislam Ebussuud's golden 'light of paradise'. By the reign of Murad IV there were 56 different types of tulip listed in the palace gardens, some so rare that even the Sultan had only one of a kind, and his expedition to Persia in 1638 was seen as an opportunity to get more. However, it may not have been this periodic influx of oriental tulips that precipitated the change in the Ottoman tulip. In 1651 the Austrian ambassador Schmid von Schwarzenhorn brought Mehmet IV a gift of European tulips – only forty of ten different varieties – but several Turkish authorities believed it was their pollen that did the trick, causing the change, including Mehmed Efendi, author of *Lalezari i Ibrahim*, which was written in 1726 at the peak of the 'needle' tulip frenzy. Nor was this the only European arrival. In 1680 *T. saxatilis* from Crete was recorded in the diary of an Italian traveller: 'in a garden at Eyoub on the Golden Horn were magnificent tulips growing three or four on a stem. They were imported from Crete.'[16] Whether or not the ghostly ancestry of the Ottoman tulip

Detail from *Surname-i Humayun* showing Murad III's celebrations for the circumcision of his son Mehmet in 1582.

Ottoman tulip from
an 18th-century
Turkish album,
Istanbul.

Ottoman tulip from
an 18th-century
Turkish album,
Istanbul.

will ever be solved, it still occasionally haunts Dutch bulb growers
when a bulb reverts to a thin, pointed, twisted form they call *Tulipa
dief*, or 'tulip thief'.

During the seventeenth century the tulip growers of Istanbul
formed a council to control the naming and pricing of tulip varieties
and to ensure they reached a sufficient standard of perfection. Tall,
thin, almond-shaped flowers were favoured, with petals pointed like

daggers and each the same size and length. Flowers of a single colour were preferred, and irregular, loose, double or serrated flowers were considered defective. There were some lovely names – 'scarlet swallow', 'matchless pearl', 'slim one of the rose garden', 'beloved's face', 'one that confuses reason', 'one that increases joy' and 'the vizier's finger' (which was yellow). During the reign of Ahmet III (1703–30) the grand vizier himself, Damid Ibrahim Pasa, took charge of the tulip scene, and his head gardener Seyh Mehmed (nicknamed *lalezari*, 'the tulip grower') wrote the definitive *Manual of Flowers*. This included a description of a tulip named 'the chosen of the chosen', which proved that bicoloured tulips had come into fashion, especially those with a white ground:

> It is the colour of the violet and the curved form of the new moon. The markings rightly placed, clean and well proportioned, the white ornamental petals absolutely perfect, the shape needle-like and decorated with pleasant rays.[17]

By this time the extraordinarily etiolated tulip was fully evolved and was also appearing in albums of flower paintings. When they were picked these tulips were displayed in vases, occasionally together in the European style, but the most perfect had a slender vase of their own, the *laledan*, made of silver or glass and with a bulbous base – one album painting showed a maroon tulip called 'the pomegranate lance' splendidly contrasted with its deep-blue *laledan*. Sultans were portrayed with *laledan* arranged on trays before them, and at festivals they were carried in procession.

Ahmet III's tulip festivals were many and notorious. His reign was known as the *laledevri*, 'the tulip era', and both the political and courtly scenes were documented by Damid Ibrahim Pasa, who became grand vizier in 1718 and married the Sultan's daughter. He was a subtle master of intrigue, and lavish in creating pleasures to distract his ruler. In springtime Ahmet travelled from palace to palace along the shores of the Bosphorus, where pleasure domes were built for him

Sultan Murad IV dining in his court, surrounded by a feast and flowers.
From the Topkapi Palace.

that merged Ottoman and French Baroque styles. In the flower beds
the tulips were planted in patterns, like carpets, and according to the
French ambassador, writing home in 1726, 'care is taken to fill the
gaps where the tulips have come up blind with flowers taken from

other gardens and placed in bottles.'[18] By virtue of his wife, Damid Ibrahim Pasa had a magnificent royal palace of his own called the *Círígan*, meaning 'palace of candles'. At night-time during the tulip festivals, hundreds of candles were placed among the flowers and hung in mirrored lanterns alongside cages of songbirds, or fastened to the backs of tortoises as they meandered through the gardens. 'The illuminations', continued the French ambassador, 'and the noisy consort of Turkish musical instruments which accompanies them, continues nightly as long as the tulips remain in flower, during which time the Sultan is entertained by the grand vizier.' In the gardens of Topkapi Saray the tulips were staged on wooden pyramids, towers and amphitheatres, and to add to the variety Dutch tulips were also being imported in some quantity at this time. Indeed the prices of tulips threatened to rise as they had in Holland a century earlier, except that they were more firmly controlled by the Turkish authorities. The court poet Ahmet Nedim should presumably be exonerated from sarcasm when he wrote, simultaneously praising the tulip and the sultan, 'And thou oh heart-expanding tulip, be never far from the garden.'

Like all foolish excesses the *laledevri* ended in downfall, precipitated by military reverses in Persia, the massacre of a Turkish garrison in Tabriz and a revolt of the janissaries. Accounts vary about whether Ahmet III, fearing for his own safety, ordered the strangling of his grand vizier. If so this was traditionally the responsibility of the royal gardeners, the *bostanici*, who would execute a treacherous functionary or concubine with a silken chord, sometimes after a hair-raising chase through the courtyards and gardens of Topkapi Saray down towards the river gate – the theory being that if the victim got there first it might mean freedom, but if the executioners were waiting at the gate the strangled corpse was consigned to the Bosphorus. According to other accounts, the infuriated populace took matters into their own hands, after which the Sultan was forced to abdicate in favour of his nephew Mahmud I. The etiolated Ottoman tulips gradually drifted from favour and were lost to cultivation, to be glimpsed only in the pages of albums or the petals of *T. acuminata*.

three
First Footings
❧

If tulips grow wild in Europe, why were they never mentioned before the sixteenth century? The Greek and Roman fathers of botany, Theophrastus and Dioscorides, breathed not a word, although between them they ranged across the Mediterranean world. Their successors, the medieval herbalists, who concentrated mainly on preserving knowledge rather than seeking it, also remained silent. Were tulips, like buttercups, considered too small and useless, or was it their preference for inaccessible places that left them unnoticed? If certain groups of genuinely wild tulips like the Saxatiles and the Australes grew discreetly scattered in the Greek islands, Spain, France and the Balkans, and if *T. hungarica* and *T. albanica* were always indigenous, then other colonies of tulips that were definitely oriental in origin were quietly infiltrating as weeds of cultivation, just as they had in the vineyards and orchards of Asia. Possibly it was the cultivation of saffron, valuable for the yellow dye it produced, that initiated this process in Europe, because there is some coincidence between the areas where saffron was grown and these naturalized tulip species. From the eighth century onwards attempts were made to establish saffron fields in Europe and, if imported tulips sometimes came up instead of crocuses (from which saffron is derived), it would be understandable that the cultivators of saffron threw them aside – and that could be how they established themselves.[1]

Centuries later, in 1753, Carl Linnaeus, in his attempts to rationalize all plants within his binomial system, named this miscellaneous group of naturalized tulips *T. gesneriana* in honour of the first European botanist to describe a tulip, Conrad Gesner, and indeed this recognition was deserved. Gesner was a Swiss doctor and naturalist from Zurich who, between 1551 and 1558, published a monumental *Historia animalum* and then began amassing material for the companion volumes of *Historia plantarum*, which were neither completed nor published in his lifetime. However, they expressed, in the words of his preface, 'the essence of the infinitely questing spirit'. The nearly 1,500 illustrations were all busily annotated with characteristics, provenance and habitat. There were two tulips. Gesner saw the red tulip in April 1559 during a visit to Augsburg (a centre of banking and metalwork in the Holy Roman Empire). It was growing in the garden of Johann Heinrich Hewart, a city councillor; 'I saw this plant displayed', wrote Gesner,

The red tulip described by Conrad Gesner, growing in Johann Hewart's garden in Augsburg in 1560, generally regarded as the first in Europe to be botanically described and illustrated.

sprung from a seed which had come from Byzantia or as
others say Cappadocia. It was flowering with a single beautiful red flower, large, like a red lily, formed of eight petals
of which four are outside and the rest within. It has a very
sweet, soft and subtle scent which soon disappeared.[2]

Gesner's description is curious, because the tulip in his painting has the normal six petals, not eight, and if it came from Anatolia
(Cappadocia) it may have been *T. armena*, which has petals that curl
outwards and wavy edges to its leaves. Gesner named this red tulip
T. turcarum, establishing the country of origin and the name 'tulip'.
Two years later, in 1561, the description of this tulip was published
with an accompanying woodcut (publication is vital in the accredit-
ation of botanists) as an addendum to Valerius Cordus' *Annotationes*.[3]

The other tulip among Gesner's collected illustrations was yellow
and had the unmistakable form of *T. sylvestris*, the most widely naturalized species of tulip in Europe, but not a plant that Gesner had seen
himself. The illustration was sent to him by Johan Kentmann, an artist from Dresden who worked in Padua, Venice and Bologna between
1549 and 1551. The label read *Narcissi lutei odorati* (fragrant yellow daf-
fodil; *T. sylvestris* does have a spicy scent), suggesting that when tulips
were observed in medieval Europe they were lumped in with daffodils.
Indeed *narcissus* and *lilionarcissus* continued to be the names applied to
tulips in early published descriptions – for instance, those of Pier
Andrea Mattioli in 1565 and Rembert Dodoens in 1568[4] – until tulip
won through as the accepted name. *T. sylvestris* was next described by
Matthias de L'Obel, Latinized to Lobelius, in *Plantarum seu stirpium
historia*, published in Antwerp in 1576. He called it the 'yellow tulip of
Bologna', echoing Gesner's Italian provenance, although colonies were
certainly established in other wine-growing areas including France,
Germany and Alsace. In 1581 Lobelius wrote tantalizingly:

It is a long time ago that in Venice and Padua we for the first
time saw these Greek and Macedonian lilies which were a

beautiful purple colour, after that we saw them in Florence and Genoa with a yellow and also a brown-red blossom.[5]

Three centuries later Robert Browning, living in Italy, paid his tribute to the seemingly wild 'red tulip of Bologna':

> 'Mid the sharp, short emerald wheat, scarce
> risen three fingers well,
>   The wild tulip, at the end of its tube, blows
> out its great red bell,
>   Like a thin clear bubble of blood, for the
> children to pick and sell.[6]

Further Italian credits for early tulip spotting include a Venetian patrician named Pietro Michiel, who supervised the botanic garden in Padua from 1551 to 1555 before returning to Venice to establish his own plant collections and record them in *I cinque libri di piante*, a manuscript of a thousand drawings of variable botanic merit, now in St Mark's Library.[7] Since Venice was a great centre of Levantine trade it was straightforward for Michiel to import plants, but again he shows two wildlings, *T. sylvestris* and *T. praecox*. The latter may have come to him from Istanbul, where it was well known in the flower markets under the name of *kaba lale*, but being robust and stoloniferous it too became naturalized in southern Europe, including in Provence, and it is one of the tulips most likely to have contributed its genes to garden varieties. Pietro Michiel's *Cinque libri* may not be the first instance of Italian art displaying a tulip. As early as around 1460 a portrait of a young lady by Paolo Uccello showed a tulip motif on the shoulder of a velvet sleeve, a design derived from an Ottoman textile before tulips entered the botanical records of Europe. Even in Flemish paintings and tapestries of the late fifteenth century, tulips with sharply pointed petals can occasionally be discerned in the patterns of brocade robes and canopies.[8] Likewise in England it seems that tulip designs, this time from İznik ceramics, may have arrived just before

Paolo Uccello (attributed), *A Young Lady of Fashion*, early 1460s, oil on wood; showing an Ottoman tulip design on the sleeve.

Tulipa agenensis (then known as *Tulipa oculis-solis*) from Pierre-Joseph Redouté's *Les Liliacées* (1805–16). It was among the tulips naturalized in Europe and known as 'the red tulip of Bologna'.

the tulips themselves, because in 1570 four men were granted a licence to manufacture 'earthen vessels and other earthen works with colours after the manner of Turkey'.[9]

To return to the type of tulip which Linnaeus named *T. gesneriana*, this covered variants and hybrids, some of which may have escaped from early garden cultivation, but all of which originated in the Middle East. The two main ancestors are *T. armena*, which Gesner's red tulip most resembled, and *T. agenensis*, which is named after a wild colony growing in Agen in France – although again it was first recorded in Italy and known as the 'red tulip of Bologna' (or Florence). Another, more glorious, Latin name was *T. oculis-solis*, and as such it appeared in scarlet splendour, displaying its black-and-golden basal blotch, in various botanical illustrations, including Redouté's *Les Liliacées*. Both these species, like *T. praecox* and *T. schrenkii*, can be variable in colour and ready to cross-fertilize when brought into cultivation. Here are some of the tulips probably descended from them which have been given specific names when discovered growing wild in Europe: *T. didieri*, an elegant pink, red, yellow or white flower with long, pointed petals and a black basal blotch found in Savoy and northern Italy; *T. grengiolensis*, a yellow tulip opening into a star with an olive-green blotch, found in the upper valley of the Rhone and named after the village of Grengiols in Switzerland; *T. hungarica*, a clear yellow tulip from the Danube gorge in Hungary; *T. maleolens*, which has a hairy bulb tunic, perhaps displaying the ancestry of *T. praecox* or *T. julia*; *T. marjolettii* from southeastern France, which has creamy yellow flowers streaked with pink and green; *T. mauritiana* with red bell-shaped flowers, also from southeast France; *T. passeriniana*, found in Italy, with crimson flowers and a black blotch; and *T. platystigma* from southeast France – especially the Dauphine – a deep-pink tulip distinguished by its buds, which are so tightly wrapped that the petals twist at the top, and it is prone to virus, which is rare in wild tulips. There are also *T. rhodopea, T. ribidua, T. saracenisa, T. sintenisii, T. spathulata* and finally *T. urumoffii*, with yellow or reddish-brown flowers and found in southern Bulgaria. These tulips of uncertain origin have also been classified as *neo tulipae*.

However, the tulips which caused such excitement when they arrived in sixteenth-century Europe came from Turkey. The person traditionally associated with their introduction was the Flemish diplomat Osias Busbecq, employed by the Hapsburg emperor Ferdinand I, whose first embassy from Vienna to Istanbul lasted from 1554 until 1562. Busbecq must have had various opportunities to travel in the Turkish countryside and observe tulips growing, but his actual recollections were not published until the 1580s in the form of four letters (packed with local colour) called *Legationis turcicae epistolae quatuor*. Here he described his first journey overland from Adrianople to Istanbul in the winter of 1554:

Tulipa grengiolensis native to Grengiols in southern Switzerland.

We had almost accomplished the end of our journey towards Constantinople and in the countryside we saw an abundance of flowers, narcissus, hyacinths and those which the Turks call tulipans . . . much to our surprise it being almost the middle of winter.[10]

Like other travellers Busbecq remarked how fond the Turks were of flowers and how they did not hesitate to pay well for a fine blossom. Indeed when Busbecq was presented with some tulips by his hosts in Istanbul, he said: 'These flowers, although they were gifts, cost me a good deal.' Since tulips do not flower in the middle of a Turkish winter, Busbecq's error of memory and dating has cast doubt on his account. However, at some point he definitely did send or bring back seeds and bulbs to Vienna (as well as rescuing a magnificent Byzantine herbal now known as the Vienna Codex). So Busbecq retains his claim to be one of the first Europeans to introduce tulips, possibly as early as the 1550s. Even in the 1540s the French botanist Pierre Belon had noticed the 'red lilies' of Turkey, and described how 'travellers from various countries, arriving in

Constantinople by boat, bought the roots of beautiful flowers in the markets to take home' – as Belon himself surely did when he returned to his garden in Le Mans, although his words are too vague to constitute a firm claim.[11]

Antwerp was the first European harbour to have a report, dated 1562, of tulip bulbs arriving by ship from Constantinople, not as collector's items but, like pearls before swine, in an unsolicited package among the bales of oriental fabrics destined for a cloth merchant – presumably as a baksheesh. Thinking they were onions the merchant ate some (the mistaken eating of tulip bulbs became a hoary tale as their prices rose), but sensibly he planted the rest in his vegetable garden. The following spring vibrant red and yellow flowers appeared, which he showed to a visiting colleague from Malines (Mechelen) called Joris Rye, an enthusiastic collector of rare plants who begged to take them away. There was a generous code of sharing and swapping among serious plantsmen of the time, and, when Joris Rye's tulips prospered, one recipient was John Hogheland, who later moved to Leiden and became pre-eminent among botanists there. Another plant collector of Malines was Jean de Brancion, a member of the Hapsburg ruling circle in the Netherlands, who had correspondents in Italy and who in 1572 received 'a basketful of bulbs and seeds of Turkish delights' from Charles Rym, who had succeeded Busbecq as Viennese ambassador in Istanbul between 1569 and 1574. (Brancion was one of the few early tulip collectors to have a cultivar that bore his name.) The tulip-growing activities of these three – Rye, Hogheland and Brancion – were recorded in the letters they exchanged with Carolus Clusius,[12] the botanist most linked with tulips, because from the 1560s a network of tulip collectors centred mainly on him. This network included aristocrats in the Netherlands, Austria, Portugal and England; merchants, diplomats and doctors; the Antwerp publisher Christophe Plantin; a Turkish governor of Budapest; and other professional botanists like Lobelius, Camerarius and Dodoens. The leading Flemish humanist Justus Lipsius described Clusius as 'the father of all the beautiful gardens in this country on

Peter Paul Rubens, *The Four Philosophers*, 1611–12, oil on panel.

account both of your knowledge . . . and the liberality which you have shown towards many'. Lipsius did suggest that the growing passion for tulips was 'a merry madness', but he thanked Clusius most warmly for a gift of tulips 'dearer to me than if you had sent me as many bulbs of solid gold and silver'. In 1614 a youthful Rubens painted a post-humous portrait in tribute to Lipsius, who died in 1606. It included himself standing on the left and on the right his brother Philip, who was a follower of Lipsius and had recently died. Lipsius, wearing the leopard-skin fur of a scholar, expounds a text while his secretary sits with pen poised. Above them presides a bust of Seneca, the Stoic philosopher and martyr, in a niche with four tulips. The two most highly prized tulips, with streaked colours, are fully open, signifying the two men whose lives and honours were complete, while the unopened tulips represent the two yet to achieve their potential. It is an interesting proof that tulips had already acquired symbolic meanings for artists.

Clusius was originally a Netherlander whose real name was Charles de L'Ecluse. He was born in 1526 in Arras and studied first at the Catholic university of Louvain. But his youthful movements included a spell at Wittenberg in 1549 with the Calvinist reformer Philipp Melanchthon; and in 1554 a rather hurried departure from the botanical faculty at Montpellier, when France was descending into religious strife, suggests he may have become a Protestant, which would help explain his peripatetic career and the unease of his time in Hapsburg Vienna. Clusius was not a bon viveur; he was a rather melancholy bachelor, but his charm, generosity and intelligence won him many admiring friendships – between 1560 and 1609 he corresponded with over three hundred different people – and, since he had no long-term garden of his own, the gardens of richer plantsmen (many of which he helped to establish and stock) formed part of his experimental lifestyle. The letters he exchanged with fellow gardeners were often about the right conditions of cultivation. Jean Boisot in Brussels (also a friend of Lipsius), who was growing tulips from seed by the 1570s (a process that takes six or seven years before flowers appear), discovered, as he told Clusius, that it was best not to move them about too much, that they were badly affected not by cold but humidity, and that straw covers were not good 'because they obstruct the air and light from which they take their force'. In 1582 Boisot's letter to Clusius records the increasing variation tulips were starting to display:

> the most beautiful tulip that has emerged this year is a multi-coloured one with white, red and yellow. Another white and

at the tip red which has come from the seeds of the white Eduarde, from which has come another that is almost violet. My sister de Tisnac has had one completely white with the tips red, and a late tulip mixed white, yellow and orange, one of the most beautiful I have ever seen. I have late tulips, yellow with the bottom part green. Voila so much with regard to tulips this year.[13]

The strong emotional attachment to plants evident among Clusius' correspondents is not surprising in any gardener, but in this historic period it probably helped to sustain them against life's uncertainties, intensified as these were by religious wars. Jean Boisot, for instance, who himself remained loyal to the Hapsburg administration of the Netherlands, had two nephews who died fighting in the rebellion which ended in the division between the northern and southern provinces. Several gardens of Clusius' patrons, including Charles of St Omer and Princess Marie de Brimeu, were destroyed in the fighting.

Among early opponents of Spanish rule in the Netherlands was Pieter Brueghel the Elder. His widow destroyed a great deal of presumably incriminating evidence when he died in 1565, but his sons inherited sketches and patterns on which they built their own careers. The painting of *Springtime* by Pieter Brueghel the Younger is based on the missing original from his father's series of 'The Seasons'. However, changes have been made in the flowerbeds, which are being filled with tulips, which would have been unknown to the elder Brueghel.

Between 1568 and 1573 Clusius was based in Malines, gardening alongside Joris Rye and Jean de Brancion, receiving and distributing gifts of tulips. Then in 1573 he was invited by Emperor Maximilian II to Vienna to become director of a new botanic garden, where he encountered the tulips brought back by Busbecq and many other 'tulips from Byzantine seed' and succumbed to the joys of listing their different characteristics and colour combinations. In 1576 he published his first botanical treatise, *Rariorum aliquot stirpium* – chiefly Spanish plants studied on his visit there in 1564–5, but with an

Pieter Brueghel the Younger, *Preparing the Beds in Springtime*, c. 1630, oil on panel, copied from an original of *Springtime* by his father, Pieter Brueghel the Elder, c. 1565, now lost.

appendix of plants '*ex Thracia*' in which he listed tulips. One of the main classifications he made, which is still in use, was between early flowering, mid-season and late. It was not until his final master-piece – *Rariorum plantarum historia*, published in 1601 – that Clusius discussed the 'breaking' of tulips into streaks of different colours, though this had featured in his correspondence much earlier. In

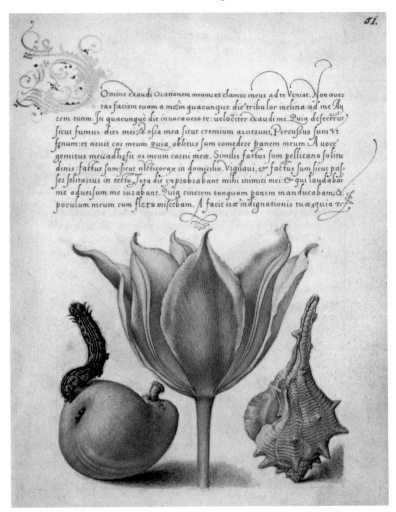

Joris Hoefnagel, illustration of a tulip with caterpillar and pear, from *Mira calligraphiae monumenta* (Model Book of Calligraphy, c. 1590), possibly showing one of the tulips introduced by Clusius.

1577 Maximilian died and his son Rudolph II proved a less congenial patron to Clusius. The new regime was more hardline Catholic, but also Clusius' botanic garden was appropriated to become an exotic menagerie, so that he was again reduced to lodging himself and his plants with horticultural aristocrats. This alienation was a strange affair because Rudolph II was a huge collector of scientific curiosities and artefacts, and his goodwill extended to encouraging the artist Giuseppe Arcimboldo to make vegetable portraits of his courtiers and even of himself. In the 1590s another of Rudolph's court artists, the Netherlander Joris Hoefnagel, created exquisite flower and fruit decorations for a *Model Book of Calligraphy* (a collection of ornate scripts), including bicoloured garden tulips. One has yellow petals slightly feathered with red; another pink outlined in white; another streaked with green.[14] Were they descended from the stock Clusius had nurtured, or did he take everything with him when he departed, with relief, for Frankfurt in 1587?

The Frankfurt appointment was at the invitation of Wilhelm IV, Landgrave of Hesse, where Clusius succeeded his old friend Camerarius to superintend the botanic garden. He had already supplied it with tulips, which he was gratified to find flourishing. The old friends had first met as students in Wittenberg and remained correspondents. When Camerarius published his *Hortus medicus* in 1588 he emphasized how important Clusius was in spreading tulips through Europe, and the following year Clusius wrote to him:

> No year passes without my handing out to my friends two or three hundred tulip bulbs which have born a blossom – but I also want my own garden to be beautiful, I would have to be insane only to drudge for others.[15]

There was one final move for the ageing botanist when, in 1593 (aged 67), he was enticed back to the Netherlands at the urgings of Marie de Brimeu and John Hogheland, who had secured for him the directorship of a new botanic garden there. The University of Leiden had been founded in 1575, only three years after the town survived a desperate siege, which turned the tide in the rebellion against Spain. The university was a symbol of national independence, but it was a struggle to establish the various faculties, and Clusius hesitated before finally arriving from Frankfurt with quantities of rare plants

Tulipa clusiana growing in the Royal Botanic Gardens, Kew (as it also still does in the Hortus of Clusius in Leiden).

and seeds. In Leiden the layout of the original *Hortus* created by Clusius is preserved – an enclosed rectangle of four quarters with long, straight beds alongside a covered walkway with potted plants. Clusius' colleagues were physicians, because this was primarily a garden for the medical faculty, and in 1598 Clusius was joined by

Jacques de Gheyn II, *Vanitas Still-life*, 1603, oil on wood.

Petrus Paaw, an early practitioner of dissection, which was to become a fashionable spectator event, making the school of anatomy famous.

In Leiden Clusius joined several of his old friends and correspondents. There was, for example, Christian Porret – another member of the medical fraternity, trading in cures at an establishment called the sign of the Three Kings. He was a refugee from Catholic persecution in the southern provinces and a keen plant collector and experimental grower; by changing their location, light levels and humidity, he even outdid Clusius in bringing recalcitrant plants into flower, and perhaps for this reason he inherited a large part of Clusius' own tulip collection. Porret's social network of plant exchanges included the Florentine nobleman Matteo Caccini, one of the main floral connoisseurs of Italy and another recipient of consignments direct from Istanbul. Also in Leiden, having moved from Antwerp, was Daniel van der Meulen, a rich merchant with a fine garden who was the centre of hospitality, book-lending and art appreciation – more fun than the deaf and irascible John Hogheland, who was nevertheless a good friend to Clusius and very well connected. From Hogheland's correspondence we know that in 1590 he produced a fully streaked tulip (*cuius flos omnia folia mucronata habet*); that Clusius sent him tulip seeds and bulbs in paper wrappings marked by colour-coded labels; and also that Hogheland commissioned artists to paint his flowers. Until 1592, when she died, he employed a professional female *painctresse*, though it irritated him when a flower had just opened and she might be busy painting decorations for a wedding.[16] Next he employed Jacques de Gheyn II, a member of a successful dynasty of artists originally from Antwerp (whose son Rembrandt painted). De Gheyn was based in Leiden from the mid-1590s until he moved to The Hague in 1605, where he worked for Prince Maurice, Stadtholder of the Netherlands, mainly producing war paintings and propaganda prints. His painting of a skull in a niche, dated 1603, is a very early example of the emerging still-life genre, which included *vanitas* symbolism. The term derives from the biblical 'vanity of vanities, all is vanity' (Ecclesiastes 1 and 12), a moralistic reminder of life's brevity and the pointlessness of worldly pursuits. Jacques de Gheyn II set the glowing tulip – which may have been grown by Hogheland or Clusius – in contrast with a grim setting. As well as the central skull, it stands in juxtaposition to a leaden urn containing smoking ashes. Above is a bubble, another *vanitas* symbol, in which various images float, including a wheel of fortune, a leper's rattle, a broken glass and a flaming heart (probably anti-Catholic). The bubble itself is marvellously reflective, a proof of De Gheyn's skill. The coins on the shelf below were also *vanitas* symbols and the medals were overtly political: the golden one shows Holy Roman Emperor Charles V and his mother Joanna the Mad, through whose inheritance the Netherlands became oppressively enmeshed in the Hapsburg empire; the silver medal dated 1602 commemorated the capture of a Portuguese galleon by two Dutch ships off St Helena. De Gheyn obviously linked the tulip with the identity of the new Dutch nation.

Many Dutch towns balanced the threat of war with a new energy and prosperity, none more so than Middelburg, where another circle of tulip fanciers emerged in the 1590s. Middelburg had been a small seafaring community, isolated on a peninsula where the Rhine, Meuse and Scheldt flow into the sea. But after the surrender of Antwerp to Spain in 1585 and the Dutch blockade of the harbour, the influx of merchants and professionals seeking the nearest safe haven swelled Middelburg's population and its fortunes. Early in the seventeenth century, the traditional wine trade with Bordeaux, and the English cloth trade, were amplified by spices and exotics from the East Indies and sugar and slaves from the West Indies. New wealth increased demand for the artists and craftsmen who created domestic luxuries – until Middelburg became second only to Amsterdam. Among the richest inhabitants were the merchant Simon Parduyn and his brother Willem, an apothecary whose shop was at the sign of the Golden Mortar. Both had fine gardens. A month after Clusius arrived in the Netherlands in 1593, Willem wrote to welcome him, sending a gift of wine, oranges, lemons and pomegranates together with a catalogue of 'my flowers and simples', asking Clusius to choose

Ambrosius Bosschaert the Elder, *Glass with Four Tulips*, 1615, oil on copper.

any he might like. Clusius reciprocated with a highly appreciated gift of bulbs, and in subsequent correspondence a group of personalities emerges, avidly awaiting the arrival of fresh wonders and meeting for discussions: 'we tucked into the copious meal and enjoyed the sight of beautiful flowers and an informative discussion about plants.'[17] There was the local minister Jan de Jonghe, who had one of his tulips painted for Clusius; Tobias Roels, a humanist scholar who first met Clusius in Frankfurt; and Jan Somer, who returned in 1592 from adventures in the Mediterranean – he had even been enslaved briefly on a Turkish ship – full of descriptions of the flowers of Crete, Cyprus, Turkey and beyond. All the same, in 1597 Somer was yearning for the tulips that Clusius cultivated, and he wrote offering a yellow fritillary and a red martagon lily in exchange for 'two, three or four of your beautiful colours of tulips'. A spark of envy entered this Middelburg Eden when some murmured that Somer's small white tulips really came from the Medici gardens in Italy. Possibly these were *T. cretica*, which Somer could have collected in the wild but which might have reached other collectors via Italy. The Middelburg community had artists in their midst who were to become famous for their tulip paintings: Ambrosius Bosschaert the Elder arrived there from Antwerp sometime between 1587 and 1593 and while in Middelburg trained the first generation of Dutch flower painters; Bosschaert's own three sons; Balthasar van der Ast, who joined Bosschaert as an apprentice in 1609; and Christoffel van den Berghe, who was still on record in 1628 long after the others had left. The same tulips that appear in Bosschaert's early paintings, especially the red and yellow ones, can sometimes be traced through his pupils' works, as if an excellent original study was used as a pattern by them all. Since these tulips were grown by the cognoscenti of Middelburg, it makes their gardens the cradle of Dutch flower painting.

Last but not least on the Middelburg scene – between 1595 and 1603 – was the official town doctor Lobelius (Matthias de L'Obel). Like Clusius, de L'Obel was Flemish; born in Lille in 1538, he studied in Louvain and Montpellier before pursuing a medical career, as well as becoming an eminent botanist and publishing important works (he even attempted a system of classifying plant groups according to their leaves). His name is not as much associated with tulips as Clusius, but he certainly knew the enthusiasts, including the early Flemish growers

Joris Rye, Marie de Brimeu and Jean de Brancion, and he claimed that Flemish gardens contained more rare plants than the rest of Europe put together. In 1581 he was linked with the production of the first plant picture book *Plantarum seu stirpium icones*, which was published by Christophe Plantin in Antwerp. It contained 24 tulip illustrations, but since these were uncoloured woodblock prints with names like *lilionarcissus luteus phoenico* most are hard to identify. However, they continued to appear, though with different names, in subsequent publications, including those of Clusius. After 1569 Lobelius, disturbed by the unrest of his homeland, pursued some of his career in England and knew the early tulip growers of London. His patron was Edward Lord Zouche, a diplomat with many links to the plantsmen of Europe, and whose garden in Hackney had a fine collection of exotic plants which Lobelius supervised and made the centre of his circle.[18] The greatest tulip collector of London was James Garret, acknowledged by John Gerard in his *Herball*, published in 1597:

> my loving friend, a curious searcher of simples and learned apothecary of London, who hath undertaken to find out the infinite sorts of tulips . . . for the space of twenty years . . . for each year bringeth forth new plants of sundry colours . . . nature seeming to play more with this flower than with any other.[19]

As well as colour variation, Gerard bore witness to the increasing size of these garden tulips, including 'a greater sort than the rest, a stalk a foot high, upon which standeth one flower bolt upright like a goblet'. Gerard also acknowledged the work of Clusius, 'at least five and thirty years sowing the seeds of tulips'; then he turned to the Bible:

> I do verily think that these are the lilies of the field mentioned by our Saviour, that Solomon in all his royalty was not arrayed like one of these. First for their flowers resemble lilies, second in those places where our Saviour was they grow wild, thirdly

the infinite variety of colour and wondrous mixtures of these flowers.[20]

Gerard may have been a plagiarist – he was accused of appropriating the work of others and making muddles. However, he did request that his good friends Lobelius and James Garrett check his work (he then snatched it back fearing it would never be published if he corrected every mistake they found). In any case, much should be forgiven because of his lyrical descriptions, which far outshine those of his more learned contemporaries.

The Garrett family arrived in London from Antwerp around 1569–70 and were at the heart of the Protestant refugee community in the City, living in Lime Street, worshipping at the Dutch Reformed Church in Austin Friars and trading in spices, perfumes and medicinal drugs (they sold the best opium in London) as well as exotic *naturalia*. The father, James senior, may have known Clusius as early as the 1560s, and it is very likely the Garretts introduced the first tulips to England in the 1570s. (There is a statement by Richard Hakluyt, writing a 'A Brief Remembrance of Things to Be Endeavoured at Constantinople' in 1581 – 'within these four years there have been brought into England from Vienna divers kinds if tulipas, procured there a little before from Constantinople by an excellent man called Carolus Clusius' – which helps to corroborate the timing and provenance.)[21] The correspondence between the Garretts and Clusius continued to flourish when it was taken over by the sons: James in London and Peter, who moved to Amsterdam around 1593 to extend the family business there and diversify into sugar.[22] James supplied medicine chests for the voyages of Frobisher, Drake and Raleigh (in 1581 Clusius hurried over to London to visit the Garrets and see what Francis Drake had brought back from his circumnavigation). Also during the 1580s, Jacques Le Moyne, a French Huguenot artist in London, included tulips in his weird picture of a *Daughter of the Picts*, whose naked body was painted with flowers including red and yellow tulips on her legs.

In their letters it was clear that Clusius and his circle felt that money should not enter into their plant transactions, which were based – like knowledge itself – on generous exchange and also on the belief that this was the best way to increase supply. Among idealists this worked, and even successful men of commerce like the Garretts kept a fair balance, although occasionally the strain showed and they accused each other (to Clusius) of meanness. The French especially seem to have fallen short. Canon Levenier of Bordeaux was a great though unpublished botanical expert. He wrote to Clusius of a tulip with three red and three yellow petals, and shared with him the problem of theft by enthusiasts who visited his garden by day and returned at night to rob him. Levenier kept a loyal servant who repelled burglars with 'good arquebuses and munitions'. But Levenier fell into a quarrel with John Hogheland of Leiden, who accused him of charging for his tulips, for which reason he sent him none in return. Even Jean Robin, gardener to Henri IV of France, and another notable tulip collector, seemed grasping. In a letter to Clusius in 1602 Jacques Plateau of Tournai described Robin's arrival from Paris:

He visited all the gardens in town and amassed quantities of plants, and so in other towns . . . but in 16 years I have not received a single plant from him. When I would not give he asked if I would sell. I said they were not for sale. I have little trust in the French.[23]

Meanwhile in Germany, where Gesner's red tulip began it all in 1559, a serious market for tulips was developing, and this was where Emanuel Sweerts concentrated his commercial efforts at the Frankfurt fairs. His base was in Amsterdam selling curiosities, and he too was a friend of Clusius, but from the turn of the century tulips were becoming another commodity of Dutch trade, and Sweert's career marks the shift in attitude. Since a stall full of brown paper packets might have failed to entice customers, Sweerts published a florilegium, a type of catalogue, in 1612, in Frankfurt, bankrolled by the emperor

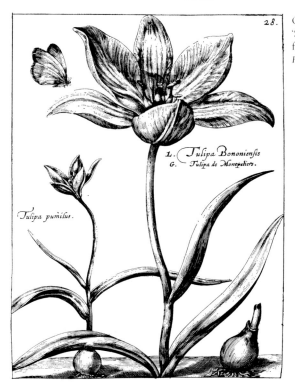

Crispin van der Passe, 'Slender Leaf Tulip', from the 17th-century *Hortus floridus*.

Rudolph II. Sweerts's tulips were illustrated in full bloom, although for colour they had to rely on Latin tags such as '*tulipa lutea rubris flamulis latis*' (a yellow tulip flamed with red). In 1614 another Dutch entrepreneur, Crispin van der Passe, produced his similar *Hortus floridus*, a catalogue of stock available from different growers, with supplements listing collectors (one of whom was the artist Jacques de Gheyn II in The Hague), which suggested the bulk of trade was between the Netherlands and Germany. Even without colour the tulips looked mouth-wateringly alive, and the descriptive Latin sometimes included the grower's name: '*tulipa Jacobi Bommii alba rub: flamis divisa*' (Jacob Bom's white tulip flamed red – Bom was a tulip grower of Haarlem). This marked a prelude to the development of individual names for tulips such as 'Testament Brancion', which was named after Clusius' old friend Jean de Brancion of Malines.

As commercial catalogues of tulips were first appearing, so too was the first florilegium which celebrated an individual plant collection, again in Germany. The *Hortus Eystettensis* was published in 1613 by Basilius Besler, a doctor and plantsman of Nuremberg with a network of links with other leading botanists including Clusius.[24] The plants belonged to the Prince Bishop of Eichstätt, Johann Gemmingen, who had created eight gardens on terraces around his fortified castle at Willibaldsberg by filling the rock-face with fertile soil from the valley below; and from 1596 until 1598 Clusius' old friend Camerarius had been involved in stocking it. The collection included several hundred tulips and Besler's florilegium illustrated over fifty. The wild species include a yellow *T. sylvestris* still labelled *lilionarcissus* and also (probably) a green form of *T. sylvestris* labelled *T. ex pallido tota virescens. T. clusiana* is labelled *T. persica; T. praecox* appears as a red flower, and another has red and white petals; *T. praestans* is magnificent with no fewer than five flowers on its stem; *T. agenensis* has opened rich red petals to reveal

Tulipa agenensis (then known as *Tulipa globosa*) from Basilius Besler's *Hortus Eystettensis* (1613).

Tulip illustrations in Basilius Besler's *Hortus Eystettensis* (1613).

its black blotch, and beside it is a yellow form touched with red – these two are labelled *T. globosa*. A white wildling with a yellow centre is probably *T. cretica*, and its close relative *T. saxatilis* is represented by a little purplish tulip with the yellow blotch shining through its outer petals. Among the Bishop's garden hybrids there are handsome streaked petals, a rich range of colours, ostentatious blotches (including blue) and even two tulips with double flowers.

Besler's aim was to represent the plants both accurately and aesthetically and in the shortest possible time. Boxes of freshly cut flowers were sent constantly from the Bishop's castle to Nuremberg, 80 kilometres (50 miles) to the north, and Besler organized a host of artists, engravers, printers and colourists to create the florilegium – the initial print run was three hundred. Luckily, despite the fact that the commissioning Bishop died while it was in production, sufficient princely patrons were willing to buy this treasure, and Besler grew rich. There seemed to be no irony in a Counter-Reformation bishop devoting himself to 'flowers, birds, gold and precious stones' at a time when wars of religion were tearing Europe apart. Perhaps he believed the wonders of God's creation mattered more than theological differences. As Clusius himself wrote in the title page of his *Rariorum plantarum historia* in 1601: 'God gave to each plant its strength and each plant proves he is present.'

four
Tulipomania

W hen Clusius arrived in Holland he foresaw where the
enthusiasm for tulips would lead and in 1594 he wrote
to Lipsius (who had already described tulip collecting
as a 'merry madness'):

> Gardening will be trivialised because even merchants, artisans
> and labourers are getting involved. They can see rich men will
> hand out much money for a rare plant in order to boast to
> their friends that they own it.[1]

In fact, despite Clusius' elitist forebodings, the connoisseurs – on
whom the cultivation of rare tulips depended – continued to thrive,
but they and their camp followers did provoke a legendary trading
crisis and an object lesson in economics.

Seventeenth-century Holland was a hotbed of enterprise. Hard
work came naturally to a nation struggling to enrich a land that foreign-
ers regarded as an unhealthy swamp. The long war for independence
instilled both recklessness and solidarity – plus an influx of talented
immigrants fleeing oppression in the southern provinces. Above all,
a huge initiative had been seized in extending maritime trade to the
newly discovered world in defiance of Spain. The Dutch East India
Company was formed in 1602, the Dutch West Indies Company
in 1621. From the Far East a shipload of spices with a ballast of
Chinese porcelain was worth far more than the traditional Dutch

cargoes of fish, timber, grain and salt, however great the added risk. Since shipping ventures had to be based on delayed payment terms, trading in futures arose from mercantile necessity, but gambling and speculation also became endemic, and not only the throw of the dice – lotteries became a popular means of public fundraising. These were organized by the civic authorities; in Amsterdam in 1601 a lottery was held to build a lunatic asylum, in Haarlem in 1606 to create alms-houses – and for such purposes they were condoned by the Calvinist clergy. Such methods of providentially redistributing wealth became widely available, especially since one could buy lottery tickets by barter. In Middelburg the artist Maerten van Heemskerck bought a hundred lottery tickets in exchange for a painting, while others offered textiles, casks of ale or weapons.[2] Tulips were a lottery too. It was very uncertain how their bulbs would turn out, but their potential rarity made them valuable prizes not only for botanists and gardeners but for fortune hunters.

The tulip connoisseurs who succeeded Clusius and his friends continued to select and propagate specimens with exquisitely marked petals which they named and publicized (the ageing botanist specially scorned the names). But how else could the variety of colour mark-ings be celebrated and marketed when the alternative was a string of Latin words, or lyrical descriptions in various European languages using terms like 'panache', 'marbre', 'jaspe', 'French marbled', 'das tirckhish papir' (marbled paper being another collectors' item intro-duced from Turkey), 'ghemarmerde', 'marquetrines', 'agates', 'agotted', 'garded', 'edged', 'striped', 'feathered', 'flaked', 'flamed', 'speckled', 'shredded', 'jagged' or 'winged'. 'Viceroy' was a name to conjure with. The flower was flamed purple on white, the finest of the whole colour group classified as *bybloemen* or *violetten*. Another was 'Anvers Bol', which was created by Pieter Bol of Haarlem, one of the richest tulip grow-ers of the age, after whom many tulips were named, including 'Bacchus Bol'. He was a patrician who employed and trained professional gardeners who then established their own tulip nurseries – Barent Cardoes, for instance, whose Haarlem nursery was named the

Garden of Flora and gained one of the best reputations in Holland. Another Haarlem bulb dealer, Jan van Damme, died in 1643 leaving an estate consisting primarily of tulips and valued at 42,000 guilders, a fortune to equal the leading merchants of the Dutch East India Company. The sandy alluvial soil of Haarlem was ideally suited to tulips and in the early seventeenth century many nurseries large and small became concentrated there, mostly along the roads beyond the two southern gates, the Grote Houtpoort and the Kleine Houtweg. Further south, at Vianen, was the nursery of Francisco Gomes da Costa, a Portuguese Jew who created no less than eight varieties that bore his own name, including 'Paragon da Costa' (a 'Paragon' tulip claimed to be finer than any previous creation). There were also private gardens in Haarlem where tulips were developed for pleasure rather than profit, such as The Land of Promise, owned by the brothers Balthasar and Daniel de Neufville, rich linen merchants; and the country estate at Heemstede of Adriaan Pauw, Grand Pensionary of Holland, a wealthy East India merchant who entertained Queen Henrietta Maria of England there and also invested munificently in local land reclamation projects. In the centre of his formal gardens at Heemstede was a single bed of the rarest tulips, planted around a gazebo with angled mirrors, which achieved an optical illusion of tulips in such plenty as even he could only dream of. But Pauw's reputation with tulips was so legendary that many believed he was the secret owner of 'Semper Augustus', the most expensive tulip of all time.

Any cultivator of a new variety of tulip had the right to confer its title, and a great beauty would inspire imitation. Among the rose tulips – those with red and white markings – an early grower had chosen Admiral as a badge of honour which spawned many others: 'Admiral Pottebacker', 'Admiral van der Eyck', 'Admiral Liefkens' – not seafaring heroes of the Dutch nation but all named after their growers. Henrik Pottebacker was a horticulturist from Gouda specializing in rose tulips whose nursery later had the dubious distinction of featuring in the satirical print of *Flora's Chariot of Fools*. A similar

The tulip cultivar 'Viceroy' (left), one of the finest purple and white tulips (known as *bybloemen*), from the so-called *Tulip Book* of Judith Leyster, compiled in 1643. The tulip cultivar 'Admiral van der Eijck' (right), an important red and white tulip (known as rose tulips), from Leyster's *Tulip Book*.

series of rose tulips were called 'Generals' – 'General Bol' was named after Pieter Bol of Haarlem – followed by 'Generalissimos' and then General of Generals of Gouda, which was sensibly shortened to 'Gouda'. As traps for the unwary there were exceptions in these series, for instance 'Admiral van Enkhuizen' and 'General van der Eyck' were *bybloemen,* not rose tulips. The 'Dukes', or 'Ducs', were named after Adrian Duyck of Oud-Karspel. Although they were highly regarded they were not streaked but were red with a wide yellow border to each petal. They proved to be a stable breed, surviving to this day in the Hortus Bulborum in Limmen and thought to have *T. schrenkii* in their ancestry. Another cultivar that may be spotted in early flower paintings were the 'Lacks', which had purple/pink petals with white borders, for instance 'Lack van Rijn' and 'Lack van Quaeckel' (Jan Quaeckel was another Haarlem grower).

Amid this variety, unrivalled rarity and beauty belonged to 'Semper Augustus', pre-eminent among rose tulips. Its reputation was based on the clarity and regularity of its markings; the flowers were purest white with a blood-red flame at the centre of each petal and the same rich colour feathering the edges. It was illustrated in more tulip books than any other variety, but very few people ever saw the real thing. According to the chronicler of tulip speculation Nicolaes van Wassenaer, 'Semper Augustus' was not Dutch in origin but was grown from seed in northern France and bought for a pittance around 1614.[3] This gave an extra frisson of lucky chance to the dream of discovering a perfect tulip, and from the turn of the century upstart tulip traders called *rhizotomi* (root cutters) were scouring the gardens of Belgium, France and Germany for new introductions and selling them on to collectors. Even Clusius, in his declining years, was unable to resist this tempting source, but since it was impossible, however expert, to judge the potential of an uprooted bulb, fraud and dispute haunted such transactions. 'Semper Augustus', however, was hardly ever traded, it was simply held to be the ideal. Around 1624 there seem to have been about twelve in existence, but all in the hands of one mysterious owner who would not sell at any price. The quoted values of 'Semper Augustus' (1,200 florins in 1624, double in 1625, 5,500 in 1633 and 10,000 in the winter of 1636/7 when the market peaked) remained purely speculative.

The third overall category of streaked tulip after the *bybloemen* and *rosen* were the *bizarden* or bizarres, which were yellow or golden streaked with red or purple/brown. One of the finest early examples was straightforwardly named 'Root en Gheel van Leyde' (Red and Gold of Leiden). At the lower end of the spectrum were the 'Switzers', a name inspired by the uniform of the papal guards. These were common enough to be sold by the pound weight, and later mentioned by

The tulip cultivar 'Root en Gheel van Leyden', the most highly prized of the red and yellow tulips (known as bizarres), from Leyster's *Tulip Book* (1643).

Andrew Marvell in a poem nostalgic for the age before the English Civil War: 'Tulips in several colours barred were then the Switzers of our guard.'[4] Another apt name for a bizarre was the 'Fool's Coat', after the traditional multicoloured motley of the court fool or jester. The link between tulips and fools increased as enthusiasm for tulip collecting gathered momentum and attracted the attention of cartoonists. As early as 1614 Roemer Visscher was producing *Sinnepoppen*, woodcuts of tulips or exotic seashells with captions like 'a fool and his money are soon parted'; and in the flood of satire that greeted the collapse in the tulip market there came prints and paintings featuring fools in motley. In 1640 Hendrik Pot produced a painting called *Flora's Chariot of Fools* (reissued as a print by Crispin van der Passe himself,

Watercolour of the
'Semper Augustus'
tulip, the most
expensive tulip of
all time, from the
so-called *Tulip Book* of
Judith Leyster (1643).

whose *Hortus floridus* had helped inaugurate the tulip craze). It shows
Flora the goddess of flowers riding past Haarlem in a wagon powered
by the wind in its sail, while in the distance another capsizes just like
the 'wind trade' in tulips. Flora holds bunches of tulips in her hands
and her carousing attendants include jesters with tulips tucked into
their fools' caps. More tulips adorn a banner with names such as
'Semper Augustus', 'General Bol' and 'Admiral van Hoorn', while
'Viceroy' and 'Gouda' lie in the sand under the chariot's wheels. A
very fine carriage clock signifies the transitory nature of the proceedings and up in the mast a monkey defecates on those below. Also in
around 1640 Jan Brueghel II (the Younger) peopled a painting of

tulipomania entirely with monkeys crowded into a stately garden enacting the rituals of tulip trading: examining a fine bed of flowers; pouring over a list of names; counting money; feasting and fighting.

Another artistic expression of tulip trading could be seen in the richly illustrated tulip books, consisting of page after page of tempting watercolours, with each tulip's name though not its price. Some were done for private collectors, others as catalogues for commercial horticulturists or to advertise an important auction. In all cases the prices would be fluctuating. Only one tulip book, bearing the fateful date 1637, created by Peter Holsteyn the Younger for a grower named Cos, did give the name, price and weight of each tulip and was clearly produced in a hurry, with assistants painting the leaves and stems while Holsteyn filled in the all-important markings on the petals.[5] A fine album, largely the work of Anthony Claesz. of Amsterdam, became known as Judith Leyster's *Tulip Book* because this well-known woman artist from Haarlem contributed two pictures of rose tulips dated 1643. Other highly regarded contributors to tulip books included Jacob Marrell, Ambrosius Bosschaert the Younger and Jacob van

Hendrik Pot, *Flora's Chariot of Fools*, 1640, oil on panel.

93

Swanenburgh of Leiden, Rembrandt's master. In their way tulip books testify as vividly as the mocking prints to the dangerous confusion of bulb trading. The beautiful rose tulip Somerschoon appeared in a number of tulip books; sometimes its egg-shaped petals were rounded at the tips, sometimes pointed, curving either inwards or outwards. Its markings were feathered red on white, with stripes along the central vein and yellow at the base. But the red colour in the watercolours varies from vermilion to purple-red, often with pink, and its features overlapped with many other rose tulips. How could anyone distinguish between varieties with almost identical markings, or avoid the fact that artists copied model tulips from album to album, giving them different names; or even including tulips that were not available (like 'Semper Augustus')? Small wonder that disputes over identity dramatize the records of the tulip trade.

It was never entirely a free-for-all, because the Dutch were accustomed to financial regulations. These were centred on the new boom town of Amsterdam, which had risen to prominence after the sack of Antwerp in 1576 and been impressively rebuilt in concentric circles of canals. The Chamber of Assurance, the Exchange Bank, the Lending Bank and above all the Bourse or Stock Exchange impressed other nations. In 1616 the English ambassador Dudley Carleton wrote: 'such are the numbers of all nations, of all professions and all religions there assembled for one business only, merchandise'.[6] Trading on the Bourse, which opened for business in 1610 (replacing ad hoc premises such as bridges and churches), was permitted only between noon and two, and official brokers had to be licensed to deal in different commodities, of which there were hundreds, from jewels to sugar. The limited hours provoked frenzied speed, typified by the hand-slapping after a deal which replaced handshaking. On the margins were many unlicensed, freelance dealers negotiating low-priced shares which might be traded-on before they were paid for. Eavesdroppers lurked about, gleaning details of transactions and their prospects. But tulips never became part of the official commodities scene, although their traders aped it by forming themselves

Anon. Dutch School, *Satire on Tulipomania, c.* 1640, oil on panel.

into clubs known as colleges of florists. Membership was necessary to anyone wishing to trade in tulips, and florists' colleges grew up in all the main towns (Haarlem, Amsterdam, Gouda, Delft, Enkhuizen, Hoorn, Alkmaar, Leiden, Utrecht and Rotterdam), providing arbitrators and witnesses for every sale, and correct procedures. One was a mini-auction known as *in het ootjen*, the small *ootje* being a circular diagram in which the auctioneer recorded the bids, and finally rounded them off inside a larger *ootje*. (This usage has evolved into a Dutch saying comparable to pulling one's leg.) If the successful bidder reneged on the deal he forfeited a small percentage of the sale price as compensation. The florists' meetings took place in taverns, and a levy was made on the tulip sales to pay for refreshments all round, which could be lavish. Artists such as Jan Steen evoke the raucous faces typical of such evenings, clouded with tobacco smoke and reckless with alcohol.

The most colourful, indeed the only detailed, accounts of tulip trading appeared in satirical pamphlets, but their exaggerations indicate the underlying reality. In 1637 Adrian Roman, the principal printer of Haarlem, published *Samenspraeken* (Conversations) between two weavers, Waermondt (True Mouth), who stuck to his craft, and Gaergoedt (Greedy Goods), who had exchanged his tools to raise capital and travelled from town to town as a florist dealing in bulbs.[7] Gaergoedt claimed to make at least 100 per cent profit, where Waermondt could only expect 10 per cent for his weaving – though Gaergoedt admitted that he had yet to receive most of the money due for his transactions. Gaergoedt's ledger contained details of bulbs he acquired for a deposit of 'my best coat and a coin on a silver chain', with an agreement to pay 1,800 guilders when the bulbs were delivered. Other deals included farm animals, a coach and horses, silver bowls and prunes, always with final payment delayed. Between 1608 and 1636 the Dutch government had regularly banned trading in commodities which were not in the possession of the vendor, but evidently deals were made for which neither the cash nor the tulips was available – 'this trade', Gaergoedt admitted, 'must be done with an intoxicated head, and the bolder one is the better.'

It was their dependence on the seasons which made tulips ideal for trading in futures. The genuine buying season for connoisseurs was between June, when the bulbs were lifted, and the next planting in October. Buying in winter for future delivery became acceptable because it was designed to secure the right to both a bulb and any offsets it produced; but around 1634–5 this interim period caused florists to turn into speculators, making a whole series of deals to enhance their profits and upgrade their stock. The promissory notes which they exchanged gave the name of the tulip, its location, the date it would be ready for lifting and its weight at the time of planting (and as this normally increased while the bulb was in the ground, so did its value). For the finest tulips like 'Gouda' the measure was given in *azen* (aces), a tiny unit used by goldsmiths; a less spectacular 'Admiral' would normally be sold by the bulb; ordinary tulips like 'Switzers' were sold by the pound. Records suggest that even during 1636 – at the peak of the tulip market – most tulips were bought from their growers by genuine collectors, but rumour and lawsuits were increasing. For instance, that spring Jeurian Jansz., a baker of Haarlem, struck a deal to buy the offsets of a beautiful 'Admiral Liefkens' he saw flowering in an Amsterdam garden, and the price was agreed according to their weight in *azen*. But at a meeting of a college of florists he overheard that the bulb had been lifted prematurely and the offsets damaged, and after making a legal challenge Jeurian was released from the deal.[8] It was between December 1636 and January 1637 that trading became so widespread and feverish that prices leapt up as never before and became known as 'the wind trade'. Even the humble 'Switzers' rose from 60 guilders a pound to 1,400 guilders, and as Gaergoedt (who by this time had mortgaged his house to buy bulbs) admitted: 'even the stuff which used to be weeded and thrown on the dungheap has been sold for good money.' It was when Gaergoedt claimed that tulips surpassed gold and jewels in value that Waermondt interposed his most astute reply:

> that is true when you consider their beauty when in existence, but not when you look at their perishability, besides gems and artistic works are possessed by the rich, tulips also by common folk.[9]

Jan Breughel the Younger, *Satire upon Tulipomania*, c. 1640, oil on panel.

A severe outbreak of the plague starting in 1635 may have contributed to tulipomania, creating a shortage of labour and consequent rise in wages, which provided surplus income for uninformed speculators; perhaps also creating a general mood of reckless fatalism. A preacher from Haarlem, Joducus Cats, wrote to his nephew that, like the plague, 'another sickness has arisen . . . it is the sickness of *bloemisten* or *floristen*.'[10] And the plague was probably responsible for orphaning the seven children of Wouter Winkel, a rich innkeeper of Alkmaar with a splendid tulip collection – 'Viceroys', 'Goudas', 'Admirals' and 'Paragons' – all planted in a garden close by. When Winkel died in the early summer of 1636, shortly after his wife, the Trustees of the Orphans Court who became responsible for the children had also to ensure the safety of the tulips. (Some gardeners, to guard precious flower beds, slept with their tulips; others installed trip wires and bells.) Presumably the Trustees were also watching the rising market, because the auction of the tulips did not take place until 5 February 1637. A tulip book was produced with 124 watercolours of the tulips, and dozens of connoisseurs and florists flocked to Alkmaar. One contrived to buy in advance an 'Admiral van Enkuizen' for 5,200 guilders, and two white and lilac-flamed 'Brabansons' for 3,200 guilders the pair. This set the tone. Nineteen of the tulips sold for over 1,000 guilders, the most unusual tulip, named 'Bruyn Purpur' (bronze and lilac), sold for 2,025 guilders, a 'Viceroy' sold for 4,600 and an 'Admiral Liefkens' for 4,400 guilders – at this time one of the finest canal-side houses in Amsterdam would have been worth a similar sum. This was the peak of the market and almost immediately a pamphlet was issued listing the astronomical prices.[11] But simultaneously other news was gaining momentum: that the Dutch authorities were about to intervene and that prices were beginning to fall; at an auction in Haarlem on 3 February the tulips failed to achieve their bids and trading was suspended.

First in Haarlem and then throughout Holland, florists (though not connoisseurs) tried to offload their stock, and as confidence evaporated the market collapsed within days, leaving chains of obligations suspended and the growers with no prospect of gathering the huge sums of money they were promised. One of the last dramatic deals took place in The Hague on 4 February, when the artist Jan van Goyen, one of the most successful Dutch landscape painters, bought fifty tulips in exchange for 912 guilders plus two paintings, one of Judas and the other by Jacob van Ruisdael. Among the tulips was a 'Camelotten', a beautiful bizarre whose streaks were reminiscent of an oriental textile patterned in wavy veins of red and yellow and known as camlet, which was woven from camel or goat's hair. For the rest of his life (he died in 1656) van Goyen was hounded for payment, and although he continued to produce fine landscapes he died in debt.

As a moral issue the Dutch found tulipomania deeply disturbing, undermining concepts of value and trust. The satirical humour expressed in a popular song, 'the flower trade is a wonder for us and

'Camellotten', detail from the 17th-century *Florilegium* of Alexander Marshal.

99

Pieter Geritz van Roestraten, *Still-life with Silver Wine Decanter, Globe and Tulip, c.* 1690, oil painting.

beyond our understanding', was sung to a traditional folk tune: 'oh what a mess I'm in'.[12] It sounds deceptively lighthearted. The first to seek a way out were the growers, moving with impressive speed and cooperation, and on 23 February their representatives from all the main towns met in Amsterdam and passed a resolution that transactions made before the last planting of 1636 should be binding, but those made during the winter of 1636/7 could be cancelled provided buyers paid a percentage in compensation. Only Amsterdam refused to sign. This decision was referred to the councillors of each city, who in turn passed it to the Government in The Hague. Despite pressure and lobbying, the authorities felt themselves above the tulip trade and – uncertain whether they were in a civil or criminal quagmire – referred it on to the High Court. The florists, though culpable, saw themselves as helpless victims of some cunning conspiracy, possibly Jewish. At the end of April the High Court referred matters back to the local magistrates to gather evidence, hear disputes and deal with everything possible at a local level. During these investigations all contracts for the sale of bulbs were suspended. Most cities reacted by ordering their solicitors to have no more to do with tulip transactions, and an admirable Dutch institution known as 'friend-makers' came to the fore. In 1634 Sir William Brereton had described them as citizens, specially chosen for their integrity and common sense, who 'had authority to call any man before them who had a controversy' and claimed that 'they mediate in a friendly manner and compose differences.'[13] Unlike the courts, their services were free. One way or another, in grumbling and compromise, hoping delay would cool hot heads, arranging comparatively small payments of compensation between growers with unsold tulips and defaulting florists, the disputes had largely died down by January 1639, two years after the crash.

Most florists did have other more regular occupations, as merchants, innkeepers, artists and craftsmen, and few were in fact rendered destitute, provided they could renegotiate their nominal debts. Despite the scorn of satirists, they were not outsiders; most belonged to local groups of friends and relatives who were in it together. The growers still had their tulips and the connoisseurs still valued the best and were prepared to pay accordingly even during the summer of 1637. When Peter Mundy (who had earlier been in Istanbul) travelled through the Netherlands in 1640 he noted that 'incredible prices' were paid for 'tulip roots', though he gave no examples.[14] Indeed there was not even a downturn in the booming Dutch economy at that time. Tulipomania was certainly a shock to the system, but on the other hand it provided extraordinary publicity. From as early as

1610 Dutch entrepreneurs like Emmanuel Sweerts and Peter Garret had been extending the tulip trade through Europe. In 1611 John Tradescant, gardener to the Earl of Salisbury at Hatfield, had listed eight hundred tulip bulbs at 10 shillings per hundred brought from Holland. And by the 1630s the Dutch were indisputably the premier tulip-growing nation. The surplus generated by the crisis was gradually developed into a larger export business with Haarlem at its centre. Towards the end of the century they were shipping cargoes not only within Europe but to North America and even Turkey, to feed the fresh mania in the Ottoman court. No flower has equalled the power of tulips to cause such an economic upheaval, although there have been echoes, and in the 1730s hyacinths enjoyed a fashionable peak in prices, followed by a sharp decline in 1737. The response of the satirists was to republish the *Samenspraeken* between Gaergoedt and Waermondt, illustrated with an engraving of Pieter Nolpe's painting entitled *Flora's Fool's Cap or Scenes from the Remarkable Year 1637, when one fool hatched another, and the people were rich without property and wise without understanding*. It showed bulb dealers and the Devil in a tavern formed from a gigantic fool's cap, Flora riding a donkey, and tulips spilling from a basket and a wheelbarrow and lying on the ground.[15] Tulipomania retains its horror and fascination and, as with all historically significant episodes, the surviving records may still be reassessed by social, economic and art historians.

five
The Artist's Tulip
❧

lthough tulips were the rarest and loveliest flowers in any seventeenth-century artist's composition, it was unusual for them to appear alone, except in tulip books and in one painting by Dirck van Delen. He too belonged to the artistic community of Middelburg, and his work consisted almost entirely of architectural scenes, but in 1637 at the height of tulipomania he painted one exquisite rose tulip identified as 'Generalissimo of Gouda'. His architectural finesse is evident in the way he set the tulip between two niches set at right angles, creating a dark showcase of geometric shadows where an ethereal light touches the tulip, the Chinese porcelain vase and the tropical seashells. All seventeenth-century still-lifes tell a story, and this one celebrates the highlights of a collection, a chamber of curiosities which would have been filled with items from the natural and artistic world. Creating such collections was a hobby indulged by many, from Rudolph II in Prague to Rembrandt in Amsterdam and John Tradescant in London, and they were much visited. A horticultural collection could be similarly accumulated and admired, but of course for this a living garden was necessary, and it altered through the year. In 1665 John Rea suggested a flower garden should be fashioned 'in the form of a cabinet, with several boxes fit to receive, and securely to keep, Nature's choicest jewels'.[1]

The story behind flower still-lifes and their season-defying variety is above all the artist's response to the collecting urge experienced by contemporary garden-lovers. Both Jan Brueghel the Elder and Jan

Dirck van Delen, *Tulip in a Kendi*, 1637, oil on panel.

van Huysum, though a hundred years apart, described travelling to gardens in different towns in search of a particular flower to add to a painting. Their vases did not contain actual arrangements (Brueghel actually wrote to a patron: 'such flowers are too valuable to have in the home'²). They were artificial displays of choice specimens assembled from individual studies, enabling roses to bloom alongside narcissi and alpine irises with tiny stalks to rise up among the highest flowers; they even altered the relative sizes of flowers to achieve a pleasing but unrealistic balance. Despite the proliferation of flower still-lifes, vases of flowers were seldom represented in paintings of Dutch interiors, which suggests they were not often gathered and displayed. Occasionally a vase of flowers was included as a symbol of opulence, most notably on the outside window ledge in Jan Steen's *Burgher of Delft* (1655), where the rich man and his dainty daughter are confronted by a beggar and her son.[3] Tulips certainly signified wealth; they changed hands for thousands of guilders and many more thousands were pledged. Paintings were valued more soberly, though they proved a far sounder investment. Ambrosius Bosschaert the Elder normally charged 100–200 guilders for a flower painting, although when he died in 1621 he had a contract to produce a flower piece worth 1,000 guilders for Prince Maurice, stadtholder of the Netherlands. A hundred years later Jan van Huysum started with similar sums, but as his prestige rose and the backgrounds of his paintings glowed with light, it was claimed that one of his paintings cost 5,000 guilders. This was at a time when the average yearly income would have been around 150 guilders.[4]

The still-life genre started to develop in the fifteenth century when flowers and fruit were included in religious scenes because of their symbolism. Still-life painting for its own sake developed in most European countries early in the seventeenth century. The earliest surviving, dated, flower still-life, painted in oils and having no connection with a religious scene, was done by Roelandt Savery in 1603. Among Savery's immediate contemporaries, Ambrosius Bosschaert the Elder's first dated painting was 1605, and Jan Brueghel the Elder wrote of producing a flower piece in 1606. It could easily be argued that the arrival and cultivation of tulips precipitated this fascination with flowers, together with the idea that the joys of the garden should be recorded, prolonged and brought indoors. In his work of 1603 Savery set a rich red tulip with yellow markings to flame among the other flowers in their dark niche, like a ruby among a collection of other jewels which might be locked away once the viewer had departed. In Savery's oeuvre the red tulip is not unique to this painting, nor is the iris or rose, but the marsh orchid is, as it balances them with its spire of small mauve flowers. Roelandt Savery's family had arrived in Haarlem in the 1580s among the wave of refugees from the Catholic southern provinces, and he trained as an artist in Amsterdam. Around 1604, when he was in his mid-twenties, Savery was summoned to work at the court of Rudolph II, probably as a successor to Joris Hoefnagel, who had previously painted flowers for the Emperor. For eleven years he flourished there, working for the Emperor Matthias after Rudolph died, studying plants from nature on expeditions to the mountains and using the imperial menagerie as inspiration for his fabulous landscapes with exotic birds, including the dodo. Around 1616 Savery returned to the Netherlands, and by 1619 he had settled in Utrecht, where Ambrosius Bosschaert had already established his extensive workshop, having left Middelburg in 1615.

Tulips were a novelty and therefore lacked the traditional symbolism that had accrued to roses, irises and lilies – and it is unlikely that the Protestant Netherlands felt much affinity for such fancies. On the other hand, Christ's Sermon on the Mount, advocating simplicity, offered a perfect Calvinist excuse for depicting flowers:

> Consider the lilies of the field . . . they reap not neither do they spin, and yet I say to you that even Solomon in all his glory was not arrayed like one of these. (Matthew 6)

It became a byword that Christ must have been pointing to a field of tulips in his native land when he said this. But in a gloomier vein, there were various Old Testament reminders that 'Man's days are as grass, he flourishes like a flower of the field, as soon as the wind passes over it, it is gone' (Psalm 103) – which could add moral solemnity to the viewing of a flower piece. When a caterpillar advanced up the stem of a flamboyant tulip, or a butterfly landed on the tip of its petal, were artists emphasizing the plant's transience? Bosschaert the

Roelandt Savery, *Vase of Flowers with Tulip and Orchid*, 1613, oil on oak.

Ambrosius Bosschaert the Elder, *Flowers in a Vase*, 1614, oil on copper.

Elder's trademark was a fly landing on the ledge beside the glass vase; was this a tiny substitute for the skull, watch or hourglass, which were the standard symbols of mortality, known as memento mori? Or were insects on flowers an echo of the Classical technique of *trompe l'oeil*, following the tradition of the Greek artist Zeuxis, who represented a bowl of grapes so perfectly that birds flew down to peck at them. Savery's flower pieces were darker than Bosschaert's – literally in the sense that his chiaroscuro was more pronounced and created a stronger illusion of recession; metaphorically in that he included larger memento mori, such as lizards, toads and, in a later piece (he died insane in 1639), a cockatoo disembowelling a toad. Both artists created larger groupings of flowers as their careers advanced, losing some of the naive charm which distinguished the early style of flower painting, where each flower stood forth, bright, upright and much treasured. In these more ambitious compositions even the tulips tended to be swamped, and in several of Bosschaert's late works a landscape background, seen beyond the niche in which the flowers are placed, introduced an admirable but distracting source of extra light.

The third artist in the top triumvirate of early flower painters, Jan Brueghel the Elder produced massed flowers as none other before or since. He produced amazing artificial confections with lilies, irises and crown imperials arching over all and with tiny snowdrops, auriculas and cyclamen peeping from the rim of the vase, while tulips, roses and peonies dominate the middle ground. No flower could have a stem that long, and certainly not his tulips. But, when their petals are viewed close up, his disproportion is forgiven for the meltingly lovely brushwork with which their streaked colours are recreated. Compared with Bosschaert, who in his Middelburg years was closely observing real specimens, Brueghel's tulips were decidedly impressionistic – but contemporaries relished the difference. In 1617 George Gage wrote to Sir Dudley Carleton, the British ambassador in The Hague, criticizing flower pieces that were 'too much ordered . . . we prefer by much Brueghel because his things have neatness and force and smooth contrast, which the other has not but is cutting and sharp.'[5] Perhaps Brueghel's patrons in the southern Netherlands demanded less exactitude and attached less importance to the patterns on every tulip petal, which in Holland were the collector's pride, and moreover worth a fortune. Brueghel was also content to include some less dramatic tulips of a single colour, known as breeders, and some of his bicoloured tulips look like cultivars of wild species, with their more naturalistic colour contrasts – for instance the green,

Jan Brueghel the Elder, *Vase of Flowers*, c. 1610–15, oil on panel.

apricot and yellow inherited from the Sylvestris group, or 'edgers' like *T. clusiana* or *T. shrenkii*, which could have pink or purple petals edged with white- or orange/red-edged in yellow. Although he was renowned for his flower paintings, Jan Brueghel the Elder did not specialize like Bosschaert. From 1589 to 1596 he was in Italy, producing mainly landscapes and history paintings, and his principal patron was Cardinal Borromeo. On his return to Antwerp he collaborated with many leading artists, most notably Rubens, so that even his paintings of flowers often included a figurative element. For instance, there was a genre known as *cartouches*, where the *Virgin and Child* were surrounded by a garland of flowers, which retained earlier associations between religious art and flower symbolism. And, in a more secular mode, *The Allegory of the Five Senses* series showed Venus and Cupid in richly cluttered settings to delight the hearts of all collectors. The *Sense of Smell* is set in a garden where the flowers of spring and summer all bloom at once. By contrast, when Rubens painted a charming garden scene, including a self-portrait with his wife Helena Fourment and their son walking through their garden in Antwerp, the flower beds were filled entirely with tulips.

Linked with Ambrosius Bosschaert the Elder's own dynasty (which included three sons: Johannes, Ambrosius II and Abraham)

Detail of Peter Paul Rubens, *Self-portrait with Wife and Son Walking in the Garden of his House in Antwerp, c.* 1630, oil on panel. Tulips are visible in the background.

Balthasar van der Ast, *Vase of Flowers*, c. 1625–30, oil on panel.

were a number of fine flower painters including Christoffel van den Berghe, who remained in Middelburg, and Jacob van Hulsdonck, who began his career there but by 1608 had returned to Antwerp. Hulsdonck's gorgeous streaked tulips, glistening dewdrops and dainty insects reflected his master's luminous style. But the most talented of Bosschaert's followers was his wife's younger brother Balthasar van der Ast, who joined him in Middelburg in 1609, accompanied him to Utrecht and there met Roelandt Savery, assimilating Savery's skill with chiaroscuro and his penchant for lizards. Balthasar van der Ast remained true to Bosschaert's pure colours and exquisite precision, able like his master to capture the curved patterns of a tulip's petals as if they were enamelled goblets (in his extensive oeuvre, repetitions occur, one tulip reappearing nine times), but he moved away from strict symmetry and the uniform frontal method of lighting a picture, adopting more adventurous arrangements of vases, bowls and baskets and a greater sense of spatial recession. In 1632 Balthasar van der Ast moved to Delft, home of another thriving artistic community of which Vermeer's father was a leading member. Among those who may have helped to train and inspire the young Vermeer, Balthasar van der Ast is a strong contender, given his skill in rendering the sideways fall of light across objects, the reflection of a window in a glass vase, and his elegant colour harmonies.

Generally, Rembrandt's art is no more associated with tulips than Vermeer's, but living in Amsterdam in the 1630s he was well aware of how significant they had become. In his two portraits of his wife Saskia posing as the goddess Flora, painted in 1634 and 1635, he made a tulip the most prominent flower in both her garlands. Rembrandt's friend Nicolaes Tulp, who was portrayed as the fashionable physician conducting *The Anatomy Lesson*, which Rembrandt painted in 1632,[6] changed his name and his coat of arms because of his passion for tulips. Before the market crashed, being called Doctor Tulip did not seem ridiculous, and he staunchly kept the name for the rest of his eminent career and passed it to his descendants. On becoming mayor of Amsterdam in 1654 he presented the Guild of Surgeons with a silver cup in the shape of a tulip, with a lizard climbing its stem, and asked that it be used at banquets to propose the final toast.

There was a lull in the popularity of flower painting in the 1640s in the sense that no flower painter began a career then, perhaps as a result of tulipomania or the dominance of Rembrandt's dark, dramatic style. But artists including Anthony Claesz. 11 and Jacob Marrell still flourished during this period. Both illustrated tulip books with the delicate precision required, but in their flower still-lifes they sought for different styles. Anthony Claesz. adopted the brown monotones of the Haarlem still-life painters, so that his flowers glowed as if by candlelight; and Jacob Marrell, by contrast, achieved a bright, metallic sheen. Marrell was German and divided his time between Frankfurt (where he first trained with Georg Flegel) and Utrecht, where he later came under the influence of Jan Davidz. de Heem, the greatest flower painter of the second half of the seventeenth century. Marrell's other claim to fame was as stepfather to Maria Sibylla Merian, whose career he launched and who, like Judith Leyster, Rachel Ruysch and Maria van Oosterwyck, proved that in seventeenth-century Holland women could be honoured as flower painters.

Writing with hindsight a hundred years later, the Dutch art historian Arnold Houbraken said: 'even before the death of Rembrandt, the eyes of the world had already been opened . . . and pure light-filled painting became current once more'. Poor Rembrandt. One could hardly imagine that his fall from favour was caused by the resurgence of flower painting, but certainly in the 1650s, when Jan Davidz. de Heem began to paint flower pieces, their vogue flourished as never before or since. De Heem was first-generation Dutch and he studied in Utrecht, probably as another pupil of Balthasar van der Ast, but whereas his parents and many others had fled northwards from Catholic persecution, he returned in 1635 to Antwerp. There he learnt to combine the delicate precision of the Dutch flower painters with the more flowing and decorative exuberance of their southern counterparts. Daniel Seghers, the pupil of Jan Brueghel the Elder, was a particularly strong influence linking Brueghel the great master of the older generation 'who could capture the fluttering line along the edge of a petal' with the newer, more vivid, style.[7] For instance, where the older masters gave prominence to the more arresting flowers of the red and yellow spectrum, using blue/purple flowers to create recession, Seghers allowed morning glories and other blue flowers to glow with their own richness. Another device used by

Detail of Jan Davidz.
de Heem, *Vase of
Flowers, c.* 1660,
oil on canvas.

Seghers was to bind his compositions with the slender, straggling
stems of small plants weaving in and out among the larger blooms,
giving more sense of space, movement and variety. These techniques
de Heem adopted, using everything from cow parsley to corn stalks
with such flair that no subsequent flower painter (even those as
skilled as Abraham Mignon, Willem van Aelst, Elias van den Broeck,
Simon Verelst or Otto Marseus van Scriek) dared escape the
influence of de Heem but had instead to follow his lead.

As for tulips, they never again received the homage that Bosschaert
and Balthasar van der Ast had accorded them, although superb examples unfurled their streaked petals across many a composition.
Their outlines had changed with the changing fashion, so that petals
with pointed tips or those that curled outwards were replaced with
larger, rounder flowers. They no longer looked like coloured glass;
instead, their petals fluttered like silk scarves, spreading wide open and
about to drop. Sometimes they swept dramatically across the other

flowers on drooping, even broken, stems. This change surely contained a degree of symbolic meaning. From the start, the juxtapositions of certain flowers seemed significant. Bosschaert and van der Ast would place a dark little fritillary, its flower bell hanging downwards, beneath a bold, upright tulip of the most garish red and yellow hues. The two flowers acted as a metaphor of light and dark, good and ill luck (the fritillary was named after the Latin for a dice box and, being chequered, was associated with games of chance). Later, Segher's and de Heem's cornstalks were seen, not as compositional devices, but as symbols of the Christian Eucharist, and thistles and brambles as emblems of Christ's crown of thorns. In one unusually explicit painting, *Vanitas with Lily and Tulip* (*c.* 1675), de Heem piled in the *vanitas* symbols – crucifix, skull, watch, shells – and a paper on which was written 'But one does not look at the most beautiful flower' – a cryptic reference to the Song of Solomon, decoded as a reproach to those who ignored the Christian message – while a spray of pure-white lilies lie aslant a streaked rose tulip, inviting interpretation. Maria van Oosterwyck played similar games with sunflowers which, though newcomers from America, were adopted as symbols of the sun, God and kingship. In one *vanitas* painting, she angled a sunflower down towards an upwards-staring skull; in a flower piece with a statuette of a crouching Venus the sunflower peers closely into the petals of a poppy; and in a third painting a streaked tulip attempts to outstare one of Maria van Oosterwyck's lordly sunflowers.

A charming exponent of the de Heem style, though still retaining some of the innocence and decorum of the early masters, is Jacob van Walscapelle's *Flowers in a Glass Vase* from around 1670. In this assimilation of old and new (fat roses like Bosschaert's and a magical window reflected in the glass vase, together with subtle colour harmonies like Balthasar van der Ast's – updated by blue morning glories and the trailing stems of cornstalks, brambles and wild strawberries), the tulip still holds sway as 'top flower'. However, its petals float wide in a way that Bosschaert would not have countenanced, and it is balanced and held aloft by the circle of other flowers, a latter-day sophistication. Walscapelle lived in Amsterdam and, when Jan Davidz. de Heem returned to work in Utrecht from 1669 to 1672, Walscapelle may well have become better acquainted with the visual techniques which he obviously emulated – but in fact de Heem's style preceded him back to his native land, and no one who wished to succeed as a flower painter in the second half of the century could ignore him.

Jan van Huysum, *Still-life of Flowers and a Bird's Nest on a Pedestal*, 18th century, oil on panel.

This happy state of affairs, creating paintings which looked so perfect in panelled interiors with wooden furniture and tapestried textiles, began to be outmoded as the taste for gilded Rococo interiors, bright wallpapers and chintzy furniture rolled in with the eighteenth century. Only the advent of a more flamboyant style of flower painting could save the day, and this Jan van Huysum and his followers achieved. His biographer Van Gool called him 'the phoenix of flower painters',[8] and to take this tribute literally one could imagine flames were casting a golden glow on his terracotta vases with their yellow roses, creamy hollyhocks and orange crown imperials. Jan van Huysum lived in Amsterdam and he too was part of a dynasty of artists – his father Justus and several brothers – all signing themselves J. van Huysum, as did subsequent forgers. His brother Jacob especially produced fine paintings, and also tulip book pages, which have been attributed to the great master himself. However, the real Jan was secretive about his methods and even resisted taking on pupils – the joyous, swaggering displays of his flowers seemingly quite separate from his paranoid personality. Tulips joined the slanting, jostling mass of flowers, with arched stems and swirling petals, streaks of colour radiating across them – generally purple on white because van Huysum seemed to favour *bybloemens*.

During this golden age of tulip painting tulips did not appear only in flower pieces. Both Rubens and Rembrandt used them in portraits, and occasionally French and English portraits showed great ladies with tulips tucked fashionably into their hair or corsages. A portrait of James I by John de Critz painted in 1605 has a background of leather-embossed wallcovering decorated with tulips – gilded leather wall hangings became a feature of seventeenth-century interiors, especially after 1628 when a company in The Hague began producing the decoration in relief by pressing the leather in a mould, so that the patterns of stripy tulips, embellished with paint and gilded or silvered, stood out most sumptuously. A seventeenth-century Scottish portrait of a Mrs Jamieson in Aberdeen shows tulips embroidered on her bodice; and most charmingly, a little girl in a Dutch

Detail of Hendrick Cornelsz. van Vliet, *The van der Dussen Family*, 1640, oil on canvas. The flowers embroidered in black on white on the girl's dress include tulips.

family portrait, filled with the customary black-clad figures, wears a stiff white dress with a black-work design including tulips.

The seventeenth-century passion for collecting was reflected in a particular genre of paintings which showed opulent rooms lined from floor to ceiling with paintings of every subject, with more on easels and stacked against tables, on which were displayed further collections of coins, minerals, statues, scientific instruments, ethnographic and natural history items, and often a large globe on which to discuss the provenance of recent discoveries. Somewhere there would be a flower painting, but generally only one. These private museums were put on public display – when the famous entomologist and illustrator

Dutch tulip tile of the type known as star tiles (because four are needed to form a star in the centre) with a golden tulip as the dominant motif.

Maria Sibylla Merian moved to Amsterdam in 1690 she 'saw with wonderment the beautiful creatures brought back from the East and West Indies' – sometimes in sizeable rooms known as *Wunderkammern* or in a cabinet of curiosities, which could be a small room or just a single piece of furniture. The furniture would be an object of fascination in its own right, with doors opening on drawers and frequently inlaid with tulip designs either in marquetry or mother of pearl set in panels of ebony. Marquetry designs displaying streaked tulips also decorated chests, tables and long case clocks. Tulips were engraved in metal on the backplates of carriage clocks, another seventeenth-century Dutch invention, and on glass and silverware. There were tulip-shaped goblets, salt cellars and candle holders. The patterns of tulip petals were a gift to textile workers and needlewomen, who wove and embroidered them onto tapestries, upholstery, curtains and bedcovers. There was also an imaginative link between textiles and tulips; Clusius, in his letters, said his tulips were like silk shimmering with red and yellow threads, and Marie de Brimeu replied that the 'tapestries of his flowerbeds surpassed those made of thread as nature surpasses artifice'.[9] In 1629 the English herbalist John Parkinson echoed her, describing 140 varieties of tulip then known in England, and 'the place where they stand may resemble a piece of curious needlework.'[10]

Ceramics were the most widespread of all the seventeenth-century Dutch crafts that featured tulips, especially the ubiquitous tiles, a method of covering large areas of wall in a decorative and hard-wearing way that was, like tulips themselves, of oriental origin. The first Dutch tile pottery was in Middelburg, but by 1600 – when tulips started to appear on tiles – they had sprung up all over Holland. Eastern influences also lurked in the designs, in the pointed tips of the tulip petals, in the grouping of three tulips branching symmetrically from a single stem and in the curious heart-shaped vase in which the tulip was sometimes placed. There were also the polychrome star tiles which had to be arranged in multiples of four so that the points of the star, which appeared in one corner of each tile, would match up with three other tiles to form the pattern, while a golden tulip lay diagonally across each star tile, edged by grapes and pomegranates. But of the polychrome tiles the very finest showed individual realistic tulips borrowed from the pages of a tulip book, streaked in the contrasting colours that made them so valuable. Other oriental influences derived directly from Chinese porcelain, which was originally known as *kraak* ware because it was carried in Portuguese carracks, but when the Dutch East India Company ships started to conduct their own

Dutch tiles showing a row of tulips.

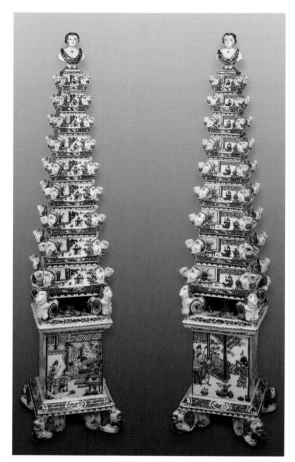

Tulipières, or tulip vases, delftware from Holland, *c.* 1695, blue-painted, tin-glazed earthenware.

trade it became even more misleadingly known as Cape goods. As well as creating an overwhelming fashion for blue-and-white ware, in which the Delft potteries led the field, various Chinese designs were also adopted. Most tulip tiles have a framing pattern in the four corners, and one known as Wan-li was a key pattern of lines and angles which retained a hint of its calligraphic Chinese origins and was rivalled only by variants of the fleur-de-lys. The Chinese responded to the admiration their ceramics aroused by creating export ware, and the wheel turned full circle when stylized tulips appeared on bowls made in China.[11]

The Delft potteries also produced luxury goods for display along the tops of cabinets and mantelpieces. Vases seldom contained flowers, least of all *tulipières*, the extraordinary confections which became fashionable at the end of the seventeenth century. These vessels came in various forms and sizes but their defining characteristic was a series of ceramic spouts projecting from the body of the vase in which individual flower stems could be arranged. The original inspiration was a Persian design, and modest enough – a fan-shaped vase with five spouts – but European fashions led to experimental creations with bulbous and elongated shapes, until *tulipières* grew tall and were arranged in tiers of water-trays, each with spouts angling outwards. Pyramids, obelisks and pagodas all lent their forms to *tulipières*, and they grew too tall for displaying anywhere except along the floor. It is doubtful whether they were much used for holding tulips, although tapestry chair coverings do show *tulipières* containing mixed flowers, but flower still-lifes do not feature *tulipières* in use. Their heyday came when William and Mary were joint monarchs of Holland and England, making their own love of gardens newly fashionable among the English aristocracy. Ornate flowerpots proliferated, and tall blue-and-white *tulipières* looked very well lined up under the ancestral portraits in long galleries. The Delft potteries created more for export to England than for the home market, and the largest collections were at Hampton Court and Chatsworth. This coincided with the time – as the seventeenth century turned to the eighteenth – when the English were turning their minds to horticulture as never before.

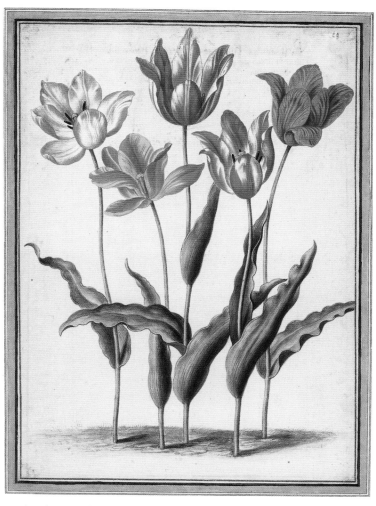

Plate showing tulips, from Johann Walther, *Hortí Itzteinensis* (1654). The tulips shown are 'Prince of Wales', 'General van Zeeland', 'Butterman', 'Scipio' and 'la Plus Belle de Brusselle'.

six

A Mirror of the Nations
⅋

I n the seventeenth century no one would have denied that tulips
were a fateful flower. In Holland their discovery had coincided with the long war of independence and the birth of the
Dutch nation, followed by tulipomania, which was a severe trial of
that nation's stability and ethics. In Germany there were the ravages
of the Thirty Years War (1618–48), when the states 'weltered in their
own blood'. In 1633 the palace of the Prince-Bishops of Eichstätt,
where the tulips that Besler illustrated had grown in such quantity,
became once again a military fort under siege from Swedish troops,
after which it was abandoned and the garden ruined. The Thirty
Years War devastated Germany more than any other area of Europe
– religious strife, foreign armies, famine and plague ravaged the
land and destroyed a third of the population. Somehow the fashion
for tulips survived, and one garden in particular was delightfully
remodelled when its owner returned in 1648 from twenty years of
exile. Its replanted flowers were recorded in another German
florilegium, *Horti Itzteinensis*, illustrated by Johann Walther between
1654 and 1674 for Johann, Count of Nassau-Idstein (near Frankfurt,
where the autumn horticultural fairs became once again a paradise
for plant dealers and collectors). The garden at Idstein was of its
time, being enclosed within a huge rectangle of walls and hedges
with niches for statues, a shell grotto and a summer house. But it
was eccentric in the design of its flower beds, which were shaped
like fruit in irregular circles. Here the Count grew the fashionable

Johann Walther, frontispiece to *Horti Itzteinensis* (1654) showing the layout of the gardens.

flowers and exotica that Johann Walther painted. Artist and patron met in (Protestant) Strasbourg, where the Count spent much of his exile, and Walther himself remained in Strasbourg, though he visited Idstein at least eight times, staying to paint the flowers during the months of April until September. He wrote how he loved to paint the wonders of nature (birds too) after living through one of the most terrible periods of European history. The slight naivety of his style adds a fragility to his flowers that makes them all the

Cornelius Johnson, *The Capel Family*, 1640–41, oil on canvas.

more realistic; their leaves show a tendency to curl as Gesner's first German tulip did, and their colours glow from the effect of gouache (glued watercolour) on vellum. Since Walther labelled his tulips, their names provide a helpful record of the various 'Generals', 'Buttermans' (and even a 'Prince of Wales') popular in mid-century Germany.[1]

In England tulips were ranged on both sides in the Civil War between king and parliament. The *Capel Family Portrait* painted in 1640–41 by Cornelius Johnson marked the end of the time of peace, which Andrew Marvell fondly recalled in his poem 'Upon Appleton House' (1651):

> When gardens only had their towers
> And all the garrisons were flowers,
>
> . . .
>
> Tulips, in several colours barred,
> Were then the Switzers of our guard.

The paterfamilias in the portrait, Arthur Lord Capel of Hadham (in Hertfordshire), had to make the hard choice between his foolish, autocratic king and the frighteningly assertive parliament of which he was a member. Capel became a royalist general; in 1646 he was instrumental in the queen's escape to France and in 1648 he gallantly defended Colchester during a prolonged parliamentary siege. But a year later all was lost, and he died on the scaffold soon after Charles I himself. The garden in the background of his portrait reflected his choice of allegiance and was reminiscent of the emblem books which combined sketches of gardens and flowers with proverbial verses:

> A garden think this spacious world to be
> Where thou by God the owners leave dost walk
> And art allowed in all variety
> One only flower to crop from tender stalk.[2]

The radiating pathways of the garden would have been recognized by contemporaries as an allegory of life, similar to the circular mazes in the backgrounds of several Elizabethan portraits. But for all its symbolism the design of the garden was a real one, because Lord Capel had remodelled Hadham as a trendsetter, with areas of smooth grass known as 'plats' arranged in radiating circular patterns rather than the usual rectangles. The Earl of Pembroke's garden at Wilton, designed by Isaac de Caus in the 1630s, was the only other innovative garden known to have had a wide area of grass cut by circular paths, like Hadham, with magnificent fountains and statues that emphasized their geometry. Naturally, since Capel's garden contained all the most ambitious features of the time, tulips appeared in the portrait and, being precious, were placed in pots, lined up at the entrance to the garden as if on guard. Marvell (a parliamentarian) certainly hinted that there was something military about tulips, as did the poet Robert Herrick (a royalist) when he wrote that for grief 'the gallant tulip will hang down his head.'[3]

In the 1630s Henrietta Maria, Charles I's queen, who had visited Adriaan Pauw's mirrored garden at Heemstede, sent the royal gardener John Tradescant to seek out the latest named tulips in

France and Holland. Tradescant (like his son after him) was a sea-soned plantsman. In 1611, for the Earl of Salisbury at Hatfield, he acquired eight hundred tulip bulbs from Haarlem at ten shillings per hundred; and in 1618 he travelled to Archangel in Russia, where he became aware that 'there groweth in the land both tulips and narcissus.'[4] At the end of his career, Tradescant the Elder was supervisor of the queen's garden at Oatlands, but part of her tulip collection was transferred to Wimbledon House, bought for her by the King in 1639, only to be confiscated by the Parliamentarians – as were many great estates, along with their tulips. (The Cecils' garden at Hatfield, which also contained plants collected by Tradescant, was described in the Parliamentary survey as 'having a square knot in the middle . . . planted with tulips'.[5]) When Wimbledon House was redistributed, General Lambert became lord of the manor and developed such a passion for the tulips he inherited that he too became a collector. It led to him being satirized in a royalist pack of playing cards as the Knight of the Golden Tulip. In 1657 Lambert fell out with Cromwell for refusing to take the oath of succession and in the words of a contemporary, 'after he had been discarded by Cromwell betook himself to Wimbledon House where he turned florist and had the finest tulips that could be got for love or money'. He also painted them, and in 1660, when the Restoration led to his imprisonment in the Tower, a pamphleteer imagined his lament: 'Farewell Wimbledon, farewell my tulips and my pictures there.'[6]

Some of Lambert's finest tulips (and other plants including a nerine known then as Guernsey lily) were supplied by Sir Thomas Hanmer, author of the *Garden Book* (completed in manuscript form in 1659), who guarded his royalist sympathies at Bettisfield in Flintshire. He had levied two hundred troops to help defend North Wales for the King, but during the Commonwealth, in 1655, he judiciously sent Lambert 'a very fine mother-root of Agate Hanmer', the tulip named after him. It had patterns of red, white and soft purple ('grideline') reminiscent of the semi-precious stone agate.

General Lambert, satirized as the Knight of the Golden Tulip,
in a pack of playing cards produced in the 1650s

There was a whole series of 'Agates', first named in Holland, which were primarily rose tulips but fascinatingly marbled with extra shades of colour. In the *Garden Book*, Hanmer wrote of the ever-changing tulip fashions:

> We did value in England only such as were well striped with purples and other reds and pure white; but now within a year or two we esteem (as the French do) any mixtures of odd colours, though there be no white in them, and such as are marked with any yellows or Isabellas [a tawny yellow] are much prized; all which new coloured tulips we call modes . . . yet new flowers with good purples or violets and white are still very dear and valuable.[7]

Hanmer listed over seventy named tulips including old favourites like 'Paragons', 'Generals' and 'Admirals'. He provided an interesting mix of Dutch, French and English names (the last including 'Prince of Wales', 'Richmond' and 'Merlin'), while other names acknowledged the eastern origins of tulips like 'Mahomet' and 'Oriental', which Hanmer categorized according to colour as 'scarlet, carnation or pink'. There was also a category of 'gridelines and douce colours', which had silvery/mauve tones and included 'Diana', 'Agate Peruchot' and 'Jaspe Angloise'.

Hanmer grew his tulips in well-spaced rows in raised beds set against walls, with another dedicated bed for rearing offsets. On a practical level he advised that 'tulips prosper wonderfully in a compounded earth of a little sand, some dry black mould [leaf mould] and the best willow earth [from old rotted trunks].' When it came to selection, 'better flowers are raised from a lusty flower of one colour than from a curious striped one of several colours that is but weak, and commonly such will hardly afford seed at all.' His pride and joy remained 'Agate Hanmer', which had staying power. In 1671 Hanmer sent a bulb to John Evelyn for his garden at Sayes Court in Deptford – tulips feature prominently in Evelyn's garden plans and notes, which included this discerning comment: 'It is not the quantity of the colours which renders a tulip famous so much as the quality, vivacity, agreeable mixture and position of them on the bottoms, streaks and form.'[8] Another recipient of 'Agate Hanmer' was John Rea, a nurseryman at Kinlet in Shropshire, who dedicated his book *Flora, Ceres and Pomona*, published in 1665, to Hanmer, 'the truly noble and perfect lover of ingenuity'. Rea described 190 different tulips (three hundred in the second edition of 1676) and broke into verse about 'Agate Hanmer', 'the queen of delight', which

> Wears graydeline, scarlet and white
> So interwoven and so placed
> That all the others are disgraced.

Rea made it clear that bizarres, though sumptuous, remained less highly regarded: 'The meanest here you can behold / Is clothed in scarlet and in gold.'

Rea also mentioned the arrival of parrot tulips with serrated edges to their petals like a bird's feathers – 'very strange in fashion' – which earlier would have been considered an aberration. In matters of cultivation, Rea recommended 'straight beds for the best tulips, where account may be kept of them', although more 'ordinary sorts of tulips' could be mixed in with other flowers in ornamental plantings. He also suggested building a folly in the flower garden with a practical purpose:

> a handsome octangular somerhouse roofed everyway and painted with landskips and other conceits, furnished with seats and a table in the centre not only for entertainment but other necessary purposes, as to put the roots of tulips upon papers when they are taken up.[9]

As Hanmer and Rea wrote of tulips (and other flowers), Alexander Marshal painted them. His origins are obscure, and he was

Jan Baptist van
Fornenburgh,
*Vase of Flowers
with Macaw and Rat*,
c. 1640, oil on panel.
The juxtaposition
of the bird and tulip
suggest this may be
an early 'parrot' tulip,
named for its gaudy
markings. The
satirical element
in the painting
is emphasized
by the rat.

variously described as a merchant and a man of independent means, but he became well established among the botanical and scientifically curious circles of London. Originally Marshal may have been French; he had certainly lived in France and spoke French perfectly, which would suggest he was another of the gifted Huguenots who found life in England more congenial than Catholic France, despite the comings and goings of the English royal family. Enthusiasts who recognized Marshal's artistic skill included General Lambert, who sent him flowers to paint; John Evelyn, who saw an album of his flower paintings on a visit to Fulham Palace in 1682; and John Tradescant the Younger, whose Lambeth garden, 'with a great variety of gallant tulips', provided some of the early entries for Marshal's florilegium – including 'Admiral de Man' and 'Agate Robin'. (The last was named after either Jean or Vespasian Robin, the French nurserymen and royal gardeners, father and son, whose careers mirrored the Tradescants'.) Marshal painted 'Chamelotte', the beautiful bizarre whose untimely purchase had contributed to the Dutch artist Jan van Goyen's debts, and 'Duc', an enduring garden variety, whose red petals edged in yellow were inherited from *T. shrenkii*. Marshal also depicted 'Viceroy', several 'Admirals', 'Generals' and 'Widows', the 'Prince of Wales', 'Diana' (one of the best gridelines) and a tulip simply labelled 'agate and jagged', with slightly serrated petals, which may be a forerunner of the parrot tulips Rea mentioned.[10]

'Sedelnulle', 'Prince de walles' and 'Rosmarinum Latifolium', from the florilegium of Alexander Marshal, created during the mid-17th century.

To return to the Capel family portrait, after the Civil War the elder daughter Mary became Duchess of Beaufort and, while her husband the Duke negotiated the shoals of English politics, she administered their two great residences at Badminton and Chelsea – and from the 1670s onwards, until her death in 1715, turned the grounds and glasshouses into the largest collection of exotics in England.[11] Sir Hans Sloane described them as 'flourishing better than in any garden of Europe I ever saw'. With Sloane's collaboration the Duchess also created a herbarium of pressed flowers – now part of the Sloane Herbarium in the Natural History Museum – and in volume 131 lies the proof that the Duchess also loved tulips. Between its pages are the streaked petals of 'Great Salamander', 'Dromedary', 'Beau Regard', 'Best Triumph of Europe' and even 'Semper Augustus', to name but a few. The Duchess of Beaufort believed, like most of her contemporaries, that greater scientific knowledge of God's creations, including plants, could lead one closer not only to understanding but to salvation.

But the prevalence and value of tulips also provoked fresh outbursts of satire. In 1710 Joseph Addison and Richard Steele published an account in the *Tatler* of a conversation overheard:

> I was surprised to hear one say that he valued the Black Prince more than the Duke of Vendome. How they should become rivals I could not conceive, and was more startled when I heard that if the Emperor of Germany was not going off he should like him better than either. Another added that the Duke of Marlborough was in blooming beauty. I was wondering at this odd intelligence when I heard mentioned the names of several other generals, as the Prince of Hesse and the King of Sweden who, they said, were both running away. To which they added, what I entirely agreed, that the Crown of France was very weak, but that Marshal Villars still kept his colours. Lastly one of them told the company that he would show them a Chimney Sweep and

a Painted Lady in the same bed together, which he was sure would very much please them. The shower of rain which had driven the company into the house being ended I asked if I might join them as they were passing into the garden. Thereupon I found that the kings and generals they had mentioned were only so many tulips . . . I accidentally praised a tulip as one of the finest I ever saw, upon which they told me it was a common Fools Coat . . . But the gentleman of the house told me that he valued the bed of flowers, which was not above twenty yards in length and two in breadth, more than he would the best two hundred acres in England.

There followed another version of the tulip/onion story, which rounded off the skit: 'a foolish cook-maid almost ruined him last winter by mistaking a handful of tulip roots for a heap of onions and making a dish of pottage that cost above a hundred pounds sterling.'[12]

If the names given to these satirical tulips have now lost their impact, they had plenty of resonance at the time. Since 1672 and the outbreak of the Franco-Dutch war, Louis XIV's visions of aggrandizement had kept the rest of Europe under threat and constantly seeking defensive alliances. The English, needing a balance of power in Europe and protection for their overseas trade, had at first supported France against Holland, the Dutch being England's major trading rivals. So the Duke of Marlborough (who by the time Addison named a tulip after him in 1710 was far too weathered and illustrious a general to be in blooming beauty) started his military career as John Churchill, fighting as an ally of France in the Netherlands. But by 1710 Marlborough had become the hero of the Battle of Blenheim, fought with great daring in 1704 to rescue Vienna and the Hapsburg emperor Leopold from a French attack. Although the battle was won, the War of the Spanish Succession dragged on until 1714, and one of the most eminent French generals was Marshal Villars, mentioned admiringly by Steele even though he reckoned the French were weakening.

The Dutch William of Orange, who became William III of England, Scotland and Ireland in 1688, spent his life as the enemy of Louis XIV. His reign as stadtholder began in 1672, when the French were invading the southern Netherlands and the Dutch had once more flooded their dykes in self-defence. The event was recorded in a far more notable literary effort than Steele and Addison's parody in the *Tatler* – Alexandre Dumas' novel *The Black Tulip*. The black tulip was in fact a myth of the unattainable – some modern tulips like 'Queen of Night' and 'Black Parrot' have achieved a deep, chocolatey purple, and in the seventeenth century 'Chimney Sweep' was one of the darkest tulips available. But Dumas (writing in 1854) bypassed horticultural reality in favour of romance, and created two rival tulip breeders. Cornelius van Baerle was a doctor, academic and artist who had no interest in politics and had sufficient inherited wealth to

Modern 'black' tulips, growing in the Jardin Plume, Normandy.

devote himself to his passion for tulips. His neighbour was Isaac Boxtel, a man consumed by jealousy. First van Baerle had added an extra storey to a building in his courtyard, which disturbed the degrees of light and warmth reaching Boxtel's tulips. Boxtel assumed it was an artist's studio until he saw the

> windows set out with bulbs, bundles of labels, drawers with compartments and wire guards against mice . . . was it not possible that, having to paint the interior of a tulip grower's, Cornelius had collected in his new studio all the accessories of its decoration?

That evening Boxtel places a ladder against the wall between their gardens and, climbing it, sees that a new bed has been created of loam mixed with river mud (a combination particularly favourable to tulips). Boxtel at once pictures to himself this learned man devoting all his intellectual and financial resources to tulip culture on a vast scale; his hands drop powerless to his sides, his knees tremble and he falls headlong from the ladder. Soon after, the Horticultural Society of Haarlem offers a prize of 100,000 guilders to anyone able to breed a black tulip, together with the honour of having the tulip bear the grower's name. Peering anew over his rival's wall, Boxtel sees the bulbs in cultivation and, under cover of night, ties two cats together and hurls them into the tulip bed. The stratagem, though very noisy, fails.

The background to Dumas' tulip story had a far darker side. The French invasion of the southern Netherlands had divided the Dutch. The peace party was led by John de Witt, Grand Pensionary of Holland (comparable to prime minister) and his brother Cornelius. They were republicans and had caused the young William of Orange to be dispossessed of his hereditary position of stadtholder and military leader. Dumas' novel opens with a riot in The Hague, a mob panicked by the French advance and the de Witts' attempted escape foiled by William of Orange (a pale figure giving orders from the shadows of the streets). The real mob-lynching of the de Witt brothers was one of the worst moments in Dutch history. In Dumas' version, Cornelius van Baerle was the godson of Cornelius de Witt, and had been entrusted with hiding secret correspondence that sought peace terms with the French and possibly discussed the assassination of William of Orange. Boxtel, who had been spying on van Baerle so assiduously, betrays him to the authorities and, narrowly escaping execution, van Baerle is incarcerated. But, naturally, he has the three bulbs of the black tulip hidden about his person and, through the coils of the plot, and Boxtel's continuing sabotage, he grows them with the help of the gaoler's lovely daughter Rosa. A black tulip is presented to the Horticultural Society of Haarlem on 15 May 1673, born in a triumphal procession on a litter covered in white velvet fringed with gold. To reveal whose name it bore would be to spoil the suspense.

Despite its pace and wit, certain mistakes in Dumas' narrative have irritated historians and tulip specialists. One was the idea that tulip breeding was a branch of alchemy. While Boxtel spies on Cornelius van Baerle he

> beheld him sorting his seeds and soaking them in liquids which were designed to modify or to deepen their colours. He saw him heating certain grains, then combining them with others, a minute and marvellously delicate manipulation, then he shut up in darkness those that were expected to furnish the black colour, exposed to a lamp those which were to produce red and to the infinite reflection of two water mirrors those intended to be white.[13]

For contemporaries, horticultural intervention was indeed suspect. Andrew Marvell, in his poem 'The Mower against Gardens', equated it with the curiosity and corruption that led to the fall of man (and plants):

Luxurious man, to bring his vice in use,
Did after him the world seduce . . .
And a more luscious earth for them did knead,
Which stupefied them while it fed . . .
With strange perfumes he did the roses taint,
And flowers themselves were taught to paint.
The tulip, white, did for complexion seek . . .

In *The Black Tulip* Dumas also repeated an error about the provenance of tulips, saying that they first arrived in Europe in 1530 from Ceylon via Portugal. This was indeed a naval route for oriental exotics, but not tulips. Dumas naturally turned to French sources for his tulip facts, and this story, like the teasing hints at alchemy, was perpetrated by Charles de la Chesnée Monstereul, who wrote the most influential French flower treatise of the seventeenth century, *Le Floriste français*, published in 1654.[14] Alongside his admiration for tulips, and his fascination with misunderstood principles of physics and chemistry, Monstereul included real observations and horticultural advice, such as noting that tulips stored in boxes for the summer should be planted in October, leaving early November for the lazy and late November for the feckless. He advised on soils, with the cautionary tale of a florist in Rouen who used pigeon dung and ruined his tulips. Noticing that striped tulips were weaker, and that the contrast colour streaked up from the base of the flower, he astutely deduced that it was weakness that caused the tulip to be unable to draw all the colour up its petals. The latest fashion was for 'Fantasticks', yellow tulips streaked with brown and purple but, as Clusius had already noted, white tulips usually produced the better breaks. Monstereul's personal favourite was Cedanulle: 'a fair violet very distinct from the purple'. The name derived from the Latin *cede nulli* (give place to none) but as it travelled the spelling and perhaps the meaning were lost, and the colours probably varied, although it remained a premier tulip of the time. It featured in John Rea's *Flora, Ceres and Pomona* (1665) as Cedanella:

Jan Philips van Thielen, *Rose Tulips in a Vase, c.* 1645–50, oil on panel.

derived from the Zeablom tulips – which are mostly a sad blewish red, very inconstant and apt to run – Cedanella is a much better flower, a good blewish carnation colour variegated with crimson, some gredeline and good white.[15]

It also appeared, as 'Sedunule', in a most unusual painting by the Flemish artist Jan Philips van Thielen, consisting almost entirely of rose tulips, eighteen in all, with a scroll of paper on the ledge beside the vase giving the names of eight tulips with little numbers that correspond to tiny figures on their stems. 'Semper Augustus' is there, as are 'General Bol' and 'General Gouda', 'Robinette' (referring to Jean or Vespasian Robin) and 'Leopold'. The last reappeared in a German list with the fuller name 'Kaiser Leopold', and it was certainly the most recently named and topical tulip. Leopold, the first emperor of that name in the Hapsburg Austrian empire, succeeded in 1658 and became another bulwark against Louis XIV's expansionism. In the War of the Spanish Succession (1701–14), he precipitated hostilities by advancing his son as a rival heir to the Spanish throne against Louis XIV's grandson. In 1704 British and German forces rushed to rescue Leopold and Vienna from French attack, succeeding at the Battle of Blenheim.

Indeed, Louis XIV had all the most fashionable flowers in his royal gardens. In the planting plans for springtime, tulips, narcissi and hyacinths were arranged in strict ratios, and in the Grand Trianon palace at Versailles there was a large collection of special tulip cultivars, some of which appeared among the exquisite illustrations in the royal flower albums known as the *Velins du Roi*. The leading artist was the court miniaturist Nicolas Robert, who in 1664 gained the title *peintre ordinaire de Sa Majesté pour la miniature*, which signified that he painted delicately and luminously in watercolour. Robert's first royal patron had been Gaston, Duke of Orleans, uncle of Louis XIV and brother to Louis XIII and Queen Henrietta Maria of England – a thorn in the side of Cardinal Richelieu (who also collected tulips) and later of Cardinal Mazarin. During various periods of disgrace, Gaston of Orleans retreated to his palace at Blois on gardening leave, becoming a genuinely enthusiastic plant collector. Until Orleans' death in 1660, it was by studying the plants in the garden at Blois that Nicolas Robert developed from a decorative flower painter to a master of botanical detail. The florilegium he produced for Gaston of Orleans reflected a true sense of a much-loved personal collection, like that of the Duchess of Beaufort, and with a similar lack of classification.[16]

'Perroquet de trois couleurs', a parrot tulip with three colours, from Nicolas Robert's mid-17th-century florilegium.

Side by side on one page appeared a red *lobelia cardinalis* and the *merveille de Peru*, both newly introduced from the New World; a pink hibiscus from the Orient labelled *mauve* (mallow) *etrangère a grande fleur*; and a most unusual tulip with petals striped regularly in yellow, red and green. This tulip was labelled *perroquet* (parrot) *de trois couleurs* and, since its petals are pointed but not serrated, it suggests that the term 'parrot' was first used to signify vivid colours in a tulip, rather than feathery petals. This may also be the case in a contemporary still-life by Jan Baptist van Fornenburgh (see p. 133), a pupil of Balthasar van der Ast, where a vivid red-and-yellow tulip, which could be a parrot tulip, is painted alongside an actual bird of similar colouring, an expensive pet, though for satirists it might be treasured or despised like the flower. The negative aspect is determined by the presence of a rat, another signifier of seventeenth-century history, bringing with it outbursts of plague more dreadful than wars and, in its surreptitious way, socially and economically significant.

There are other parrot tulips in Robert's florilegium, and the best is labelled *perroquet flamboyant*, with beautiful pink and green petals – more like a modern viridiflora tulip with the green colour up the centre of each petal. The petals are slender and pointed, fanning outwards gracefully and slightly serrated. But, since the common feature of Gaston of Orleans' parrot tulips is their green streak, the idea behind their naming remains unclear – unless it be that the first parrots introduced into Europe were green. Gaston of Orleans, like a true botanist, seems to have valued species tulips as well. *T. saxatilis* appears, labelled *tulipe de Crete*; and two red *T. shrenkii*, one edged with yellow and both with their yellow basal blotches glowing through, are labelled *tulipes communes*. Among Gaston's streaked tulips, mostly known in French as *panachée, fouettée* or *burinée*, are several quite unlike the usual mode. One, called *abricot panaché*, is subtly shaded in orangey pinks and yellows, with just a few irregular streaks and spots, the outstanding feature being the twist of its pointed petals. Another tulip has no label and is large but not streaked in any usual way, having irregular areas of red, yellow and white like a summer pudding served with cream. As his career advanced, Nicolas Robert's work became less decorative and more scientific. He worked not only for Louis XIV but for the Académie Royale des Sciences. His plants were sometimes depicted complete with roots, seeds and seedcases, making him an early exponent of eighteenth-century developments in botanical illustration.

Among the many unpleasant aspects of Louis XIV's long reign was the renewed persecution of Huguenots, whose religious convictions had been tolerated in France since the Edict of Nantes in 1598, until Louis XIV revoked it in 1685. Tulips had mapped the movement of refugees from religious intolerance ever since their first arrival in sixteenth-century Holland and England. Later, Huguenot refugees from Louis XIV's France filled the regiments which William of

Tulips from Nicolas Robert's florilegium, including one with markings similar to summer pudding served with cream.

Detail from the Stoke Edith wall hanging, 1710–20, embroidered linen canvas with silk and wool. The formal beds are planted with tulips.

Orange brought to England in 1688 when he successfully relieved James II of his crown. During the Catholic insurgency which followed in Ireland, when James attempted to return, William III's victory at the Battle of the Boyne in 1690 owed much to Huguenot officers. And when the Dublin Florists' Society was founded in 1746, its tulip-growing origins could be traced to those same officers who had settled in Ireland.

The colonization of North America by settlers from Holland, England, France and Germany was also interwoven with the search for religious freedom. It was mainly the early Dutch settlers of New Amsterdam who introduced tulips, and grew them in the soil that now lies under the avenues of Manhattan. Adriaen van der Donck, who settled there in 1642, described the vegetables and flowers that his countrymen succeeded in raising, including tulips. The last Dutch governor of New Amsterdam was Peter Stuyvesant, who built Wall

Street as a defence against rival colonies. But when the settlement was ceded to the English in 1664, and renamed New York, Stuyvesant retired and grew tulips on his property, known as the Bowery and now a neighbourhood of Manhattan approached along Stuyvesant Street. The annual American tulip festivals held in various places with Dutch heritage, from Albany in New York to Michigan, were founded in the mid-twentieth century, but their origins have been traced back to the *Pinksterfest* (Dutch for Pentecost or Whitsun), which was a religious holiday for the early settlers that coincided with tulip flowering. For the settlers' African slaves it became a few days of freedom when they could visit family members who had been sold to other properties. By the nineteenth century *Pinksterfest* had evolved into a large urban celebration of African culture and carnival, and for fear of riots it was banned in 1811 – until its revival as a tulip festival.

A small and relatively benign reminder of the movement of peoples and tulips appears in the Stoke Edith tapestry, created around 1710–20. In this Anglo-Dutch-style garden a black servant – most fashionable at the time – waits in the shadows to attend the gentlemen and ladies admiring the beds of tulips, which are lined up formally to correspond with the geometry of the garden.

seven

Botanists and Florists

꧁

I n the eighteenth century tulips lost their pre-eminence in horticultural collections, being rivalled by so many new exotics which had arrived as European trade and colonization grew to reach across all points of the globe. These fresh variations of plant form and behaviour stimulated great advances in scientific enquiry, which for botanists centred on the work of Carl Linnaeus and his sexual system of plant classification. Naturally the shift of emphasis was reflected in the careers of the botanical illustrators of the period, starting with Maria Sibylla Merian. Her training as a flower painter began in Frankfurt, where she was both the daughter and wife of artists; Jacob Marrel, who illustrated tulip books, was her stepfather, and Abraham Mignon (Jan Davidz. de Heem's best imitator) was a fellow apprentice. Her *New Book of Flowers*, published in three volumes between 1675 and 1680, was intended as a model book for her painting and embroidery classes, until its popularity established her reputation – small wonder because the contrasting colours of her tulips glowed like satin, her leaves and petals quivered with life, and she included novelties like feathery parrot tulips. After moving to Holland, Merian became increasingly intrigued by the interaction of plants and insects, and at the turn of the century she departed intrepidly for the Dutch sugar colony of Surinam to study the matter in the tropics – the resultant publication was *Metamorphosis insectorum* (1705), but there were no more tulips.

George Ehret's even more spectacular career began more humbly as a gardener's apprentice and son of a gardener near Heidelberg. But by 1728, when he was twenty years old, Ehret was working at Karlsruhe, the fabulous garden of the Margrave of Baden Wurttemberg. During the period of tulipomania an earlier margrave had produced an inventory of 4,796 tulips, a number not to be equalled, but in 1715 the new Margrave, Karl Wilhelm III, rebuilt his gardens with large,

Maria Sybilla Merian, Tulip 'Diana', one of the finest late 17th-century cultivars, from the *Neues Blumenbuch* (New Book of Flowers, 1680).

Georg Ehret,
'Parrot Tulip',
from the *Karlsruhe
Tulpenbuch* (1730).

complex parterres, and the lists for the period when George Ehret was gardener numbered a collection of over 2,000 tulips, and increasing. The Margrave's florilegium, the *Karlsruher Tulpenbuch* (1730), channelled the artistic talents of his young gardener to new and extraordinary effect, Ehret's tulip illustrations proving that the new vitality was not lost when Merian left for the tropics. Indeed, Ehret produced an even more breathtaking illustration of a parrot tulip, although they were still not universally admired in the early eighteenth century. Van Oosten in *The Dutch Gardener* (1703), a work full of cultivation notes and prejudice, praised tulips as the 'Queen of Flowers' but dismissed parrot tulips as 'monsters frightful to look upon'. After Karlsruhe, Ehret proceeded to work alongside all the most important botanists of his time and is credited with painting thousands of tulips during his career. In Nuremberg he formed a lifelong working partnership with Jacob Trew, the physician, plant collector and publisher. In Paris Ehret worked at the Jardin des Plantes alongside Bernard Jussieu. In London, where he settled after 1736, he worked closely with Sir Hans Sloane and Philip Miller (whose sister-in-law he married) at the Chelsea Physic Garden. And he also became a great favourite with the Duchess of Portland, a rich and avid collector, bluestocking and scientist, who filled her gardens at Bulstrode in Buckinghamshire with the latest plants and entertained interested parties on a grand scale. There Ehret met Mrs Delany, creator of the delicate 'flower mosaics', who was the Duchess's constant companion. In October 1768 Mrs Delany wrote sympathetically in her diary: 'poor Ehret begins to complain of his eyes, he has hurt them with inspecting leaves and flowers in the microscope in order to dissect them'[1] – a fascinating if slightly misdirected comment, because it was surely the reproductive parts of flowers that Ehret was dissecting. The most scientifically important collaboration of Ehret's life was with Linnaeus himself, and as the latter's theories gained acceptance most serious botanical illustrations, like Ehret's, included necessary diagrams of the stamens and pistils alongside the plant itself. The two men met in 1735 – early in both their careers – when they were working in the garden of George Cliffort, a wealthy Amsterdam banker and plant collector with a garden at Heemstede outside Haarlem. While Linnaeus was Cliffort's garden manager he compiled a descriptive catalogue of the plant collection, *Hortus cliffortianus* (1738), using the opportunity to publish his new sexual classification system for the first time. For this, Ehret supplied twenty plates, complete with details of the inner floral parts.

Linnaeus proposed his theory more fully in *Systemae naturae* (first published in 1735 and in its entirety in 1758), explaining how to classify plants by counting their male stamens and female pistils. The system started with the apparently monogamous canna, which has just one of each, and proceeded to upset polite eighteenth-century society with the apparent profligacy of multiple male and female organs concealed within innocent petals. Tulips, like other members of the lily family, normally number six stamens and one pistil, a situation described as one female, many males. Linnaeus' other less controversial innovation, the binomial system, distinguished each plant by just two Latin names, the genus (such as *Tulipa*) and species (for example, *sylvestris* or *clusiana*). By the time this was published in 1753 Linnaeus had named and classified well over 7,000 plants, and the chaotic practice of tagging extra Latin names onto every newly discovered flower was abandoned. Latin was still the lingua franca of Europe, but that did not mean it was accessible to all potential readers. The task of translating Linnaeus into English was undertaken by Erasmus Darwin, grandfather of Charles and a far more colourful character. He was a doctor so renowned in his Lichfield practice that George III invited him, unavailingly, to London. In the Midlands, Darwin was a friend of many who drove the Industrial Revolution, including Josiah Wedgwood, Matthew Boulton and James Watt; he was a bon viveur and affectionate family man who was passionately opposed to the slave trade, and among many other pursuits he cultivated a botanic garden.

Erasmus Darwin arrived at the theory of evolution by 1770 and proposed it openly, but not through the detailed case studies with which his grandson shocked Victorian society. Erasmus wrote poetry and this was how, after translating Linnaeus, he set about popularizing a huge amount of botanical knowledge 'for ladies and other unemployed scholars'. Two of his long poems were called *The Economy of Vegetation* (1791, in which he suggested the earth was formed from a cosmic explosion and that organic life began in the sea) and *The Loves of the Plants* (1789, about individual flowers). The latter was the taxonomic poem; it opened with a chart of the Linnaean sexual system headed 'The Marriage of Plants', and its verses contained a great variety of botanical information. With tulips it was the overwintering bulb that most struck Darwin:

When o'er the cultured lawns and dreary wastes
Retiring Autumn flings her howling blasts . . .

In withering heaps collects the flowery spoil,
And each chill insect sinks beneath the soil;
Quick flies fair Tulipa the loud alarms,
And folds her infant closer in her arms;
In some lone cave, secure pavilion, lies,
And waits the courtship of serener skies.

If this seems cloyingly unscientific, the balance was redressed by the note that followed on the nature of bulbs, describing the underground storage organ formed from the stem:

These bulbs in every respect resemble buds except in their being produced underground, and include the leaves and flower in miniature, which are to be expanded in the ensuing spring. By cautiously cutting through the concentric coats of a tulip root . . . the whole flower is beautifully seen by the naked eye with its petals, pistil and stamens.[2]

In the eighteenth century a fascination with the Greek and Roman foundations of botany remained strong. In 1784 John Sibthorpe, son of a professor of botany at Oxford, resolved to travel to Greece and Turkey in search of the medicinal plants mentioned by Dioscorides. He stopped first in Vienna to study the oldest remaining text (the *Codex Vindobonensis* that Osias Busbecq had acquired in Istanbul) and while there he persuaded Ferdinand Bauer, at the start of his career as a botanical illustrator, to accompany him. Within the twelve magnificent volumes of *Flora Graeca* that resulted from their travels is an exquisite little *T. clusiana* that they found growing wild in Turkey.[3] Its solitariness marked how tulips had lost their importance among investigative botanists, although the entire work indicated a significant shift towards concentrating on the wild origins of plants. This was also evident in Pierre Joseph Redouté's last and greatest work, *Les Liliacées*, compiled for Empress Josephine to record her wondrous collection at Malmaison and published from 1802 to 1816 (almost simultaneously with *Flora Graeca*).[4] Where Sibthorpe had researched the plants of a particular region, Redouté followed another scientific innovation by concentrating on a particular plant family, though he used 'lily' in its widest sense, and ranged through recently introduced monocotyledons from ginger to kniphofia and orchids. Among Redouté's tulips were two bicoloured cultivars named according to the Linnaean system *T. gesneriana* (a catch-all for tulips reared in Europe). But the rest were wild species that had come into the empress's collection: *T. clusiana, T. sylvestris, T. celsiana (sylvestris's* smaller relative), *T. agenensis* (then called *T. oculis-solis*, shown with one petal turned elegantly down to reveal its black-and-golden blotch) and *T. schrenkii* (then known as *T. suaveolens* for its sweet scent). Finally, in the eighth volume, towards the end of the great work, since it had very recently arrived at Malmaison, came *T. acuminata* (then alternatively called *T. cornuta*), with its uniquely thread-like petals, red and yellow, pointed and slightly twisting – posing the riddle whether the Ottoman tulip had developed from this species or vice versa; or whether it should have a specific name at all, if it was really a curious hybrid. However, it retains the name *T. acuminata* which it was given in 1811, when the type specimen arrived at the Copenhagen Botanic Garden.

The identification of increasing numbers of tulip species was chronicled and illustrated in *Curtis's Botanical Magazine*, begun in 1787 by the Lambeth nurseryman and entrepreneur William Curtis and continuing ever since. It was intended as an illustrated periodical to familiarize a wider audience of readers with all the new ornamental and exotic plants, giving descriptions, provenance and cultivation notes, and – because of its close links with Kew Gardens and leading plantsmen – it flourished. Many of the early botanical illustrations were by James Sowerby, the foremost English practitioner of the genre – skilful, prolific but above all the pioneer of printing techniques that made colour plates economically viable (the young Redouté sought Sowerby's instruction during his visit to England in 1787). However, even the canny Sowerby risked overstretching

Tulipa sylvestris from
Pierre-Joseph
Redouté's *Les Liliacées*
(1805–16).

his resources with publications that did not sell in sufficient numbers
– for instance *The Florist's Delight*, which had plates of the latest tulip
cultivars. And the unfortunate Robert Thornton bankrupted himself
producing the elephantine *The Temple of Flora* (1799–1807) just as
Europe was plunged into the French Revolutionary Wars. The full
title of Thornton's work, designed to lure the botanically minded, was
New Illustrations of the Sexual System of Linnaeus, but the famous coloured
plates were in a separate volume, commissioned from leading, but

Tulips from Robert Thornton, *Temple of Flora* (1799–1807), taken from a painting by Philip Reinagle. The top tulip is 'Louis XVI', directly beneath is 'General Washington', and below centre, 'La Majestieuse'; to the left are 'La Triomphe Royale' (red) and 'Gloria Mundi' (yellow); to the right, 'Duchess of Devonshire' and 'Earl Spencer'.

not botanical, artists with no expense spared in their reproduction. They have captured the imagination ever since by placing the flowers towering over picturesque settings – the tulips in a Dutch landscape with water, a small town and a windmill – that are evocative and faintly absurd, with an accompanying text that unintentionally sounds much like Steele and Addison's satire in the *Tatler* a century earlier:

Most prominent, a tulip named after that unfortunate French monarch Louis XVI, then in the meridian of his glory, the edges of whose petals are stained with black, which is the true emblem of sorrow . . . the next tulip in dignity has petals of a firmer structure bordered in dark purple named after the man *justum et tenacem propositi* General Washington. Beneath is La Majestieuse; the carnation tulip is La Triomphe Royale; beneath is Gloria Mundi whose yellow ground is an emblem of sublunary perfection. The two remaining tulips have been newly raised by Davey and Mason, and were named by me after two very distinguished patrons of this work, her grace the Duchess of Devonshire, for her fine sense and expressive beauty, and Earl Spencer for his memorable conduct of our navy.[5]

The last two tulips listed in Thornton's florid description were English florists' tulips, reared by two London nurserymen, Thomas Davey in the Kings Road, Chelsea, and John Mason in Fleet Street. The word florist went through various vicissitudes, often with a snobbish element, before settling down around 1870 to indicate the cut-flower trade. Early on the Dutch, by blaming *floristen* for tulipomania, risked bringing the new word into disrepute, but at the same time the English were starting to use 'florist' to denote plant specialists. In 1629 John Parkinson used the term in his herbal *Paradisus* for people who grew plants for their beauty rather than utility. In 1682 Samuel Gilbert, rector and plantsman (the son-in-law of John Rea and heir to Rea's tulip collection) wrote the very successful *Florists' Vade Mecum*, the first book to use the word in its title. Among his listings and plant notes he too expressed elitism by dismissing 'the trifles adored among countrywomen but of no esteem to a florist who is taken up with things of more value'.[6] Specializing in perfecting one type of flower was the heart of the matter; holding convivial meetings and organizing competitions encouraged it no end, and the participation of working-class enthusiasts became a feature.

Written evidence of seventeenth-century florists' societies in England is sketchy; for instance in 1677 William Lucas, a London nurseryman with premises near the Strand, made a will bequeathing the cost of a gold ring to every member of the Society of Florists (their tulips and their feasts being left to the imagination). The first recorded florists' feast was held in Norwich in May 1631. It attracted the disapproval of local puritans on account of the carousing and because the proceedings were dedicated to the goddess Flora, who seemed to be undermining Christian morals. In response to these mutterings the Bishop's chaplain and others wrote in defence of the florists, and their words made it clear that the flowers in question were indeed tulips. Possibly the early concentration of tulip growing in Norwich and East Anglia was due not only to the suitable soil but to sizeable settlements of Flemish and Huguenot weavers and Dutch water engineers, bringing not only the flowers themselves but the acceptability of including manual workers in florists' societies, along-side the landed and professional classes. (Certainly at this time there were florists' societies in Dutch and Flemish towns.) In York the earliest surviving record of a florists' society is a copperplate used to create invitations to meetings which bears the arms of Queen Anne and therefore dates between 1702 and 1714. From then on the growth of local newspapers coincided with the development of florists' societies and recorded their activities. In 1716 a piece in *Memoirs of Gardening* explained:

> The tulips with pointed petals at top, as the Mourning Widow or Fools Coat, are not now esteemed. Those whose petals are broad and round at top are most valued and whose cups open well, and which are white at bottom of the purplish sort.[7]

Thus the criteria for the English florists' tulips were being set, and no less a personage than Philip Miller of the Chelsea Physic Garden weighed in. He was also president of the Botanical Society

Tulips in beer bottles, on display at an annual show of the Wakefield
and North of England Tulip Society.

of London, which met every week at the Rainbow Coffee House
in Watling Street to discuss such matters as the cause of breaking
in tulips. In 1724 the first edition of his great work appeared as *The
Gardeners' and Florists' Dictionary* (and *Florists'* was later dropped), giving
the properties of florists' tulips:

> a tall strong stem and petals that when open stand erect. The
> bottom of the flower should be proportioned to the top, the
> upper part rounded and not pointed, and the stripes should
> be small and regular, arising quite from the bottom.

Miller explained that, if the base 'remained self-coloured', the stripes might disappear again. He made every effort to encourage home-grown tulips:

> There are some curious persons who have lately obtained many valuable breeders from seeds sown in England, and if we were as industrious as the people of France and Flanders we might in a few years have as great a variety as is to be found in any part of Europe.[8]

On the other hand, in eighteenth-century Scotland the leading tulip enthusiast was James Justice, an eminent Edinburgh lawyer and fellow of the Royal Society who spent a fortune on *bybloemens* from the Haarlem nurseries. Their names were indicative of colonialist expansion – 'Rex Indiarum', 'Reine de Congo', 'Konig van Siam'

Florists' tulips growing in allotments in Wakefield.

– and Justice endeavoured to keep them thriving with a shipload of imported Dutch soil.

By the mid-eighteenth century newspaper notifications of florists' feasts proved that there were societies springing up all over the country and holding competitions for the finest blooms. These took place in pubs, and the prizes were copper kettles, silver punch ladles or pieces of plate. A contemporary commented: 'at these exhibitions let not the gardeners be dejected if a weaver runs away with the prize, as is often done.'[9] With the growth of industry, membership became increasingly urban – ironmasters, gunsmiths, railwaymen; in Wakefield it was shoemakers; in Sheffield cutlers; in Nottingham lacemakers; in the potteries of Stoke, Worcester, Derby and Swansea, florists' tulips appeared on the china their craftsmen painted and grew. Some factory workers had their own small, smoky gardens, but many florists' tulips were grown on allotments. Several members of the one remaining society, the Wakefield and North of England Tulip Society, still cultivate their tulips on allotments, planting them in early November in the soil where potatoes have grown, so that the ground is well dug and the fertilizer given to the potatoes has matured and been partially absorbed. Ever since 1761, when Matthew Boulton endowed the Birmingham allotments, philanthropic manufacturers began to realize the link between health and efficiency in their workers, and provided plots of land for outdoor pursuits away from tenements and pubs.

Nineteenth-century florists' tulips were often the darlings of 'men of very humble condition, who devote their short minutes of leisure to such a pursuit'.[10] The most famous was Tom Storer, a railway fitter, who grew his tulips along the embankments of Derby's railways and was responsible for breeding at least three of the outstanding florists' tulips that are still in existence and winning prizes. The first was 'Dr Hardy', named after a doctor and alderman of Manchester who was formidable in setting the standards by which tulips should be judged. The tulip Dr Hardy himself produced was 'Talisman', a beautiful *bybloemen* emerging from a dull purple breeder to rival the *bybloemens*

'Dr Hardy', a florists' tulip from the Wakefield and North of England Tulip Society.

that still bore French names like 'Louis XVI' and *Habit de Noces*. The tulip Tom Storer named 'Dr Hardy' was initially a breeder (they always are) which broke in 1862, described as 'rich chestnut red with a bright yellow base, easily recognisable by the dark brown marking on the stem below the petals'.[11] Another tulip Tom Storer raised was 'Sam Barlow,' a cross between 'Dr Hardy' and 'Sir Joseph Paxton'. The latter was first bred in 1845 and named after the eminent head gardener at Chatsworth – the names of several florists' tulips reflect the patronage of the Dukes of Devonshire and other members of the Cavendish family. Likewise Lord Stanley, Earl of Derby, after whom the third of Tom Storer's bizarre tulips was named, and Lady Stanhope, whose name was given to a rosy purple *bybloemen* reared by John Pearson, a Nottingham stocking maker and tulip breeder, were also patrons of tulip growers. The tulip named after Joseph Paxton is described as 'maroon black on a lemon yellow ground, late to bloom and a poor increaser'. However, Tom Storer did the trick, crossing it with 'Dr Hardy' to produce 'Sam Barlow' around 1860:

easily recognised by a large twisted stigma; it produces a superb flame flower and less frequently a feather. Mahogany brown on a yellow base, and deep red-brown in its broken forms, a strong grower and making good increase.

The real Sam Barlow was a Rochdale man, first employed in a bleach works and rising to own the firm. He became magistrate, alderman and president of Manchester Arts Club. Somehow he found the time to collect all the flowers that in Victorian times were known as florists' flowers — tulips, auriculas, polyanthus, pinks, pansies and chrysanthemums — until he became known as 'king of the northern florists'. He had four show tulip beds, each with 140 rows of seven flowers. One of his finest was 'Annie McGregor', a rich rose pink on a pure white base, raised by the Lancashire weaver John Martin around

'Sir Joseph Paxton', a florists' tulip from the Wakefield and North of England Tulip Society.

1856, a sister seedling to 'Mabel', a softer rose-pink and white and 'better at multiplying'. Barlow was a ruthless collector – to obtain 'Mrs Jackson', a fine *bybloemen* bred by the silk weaver David Jackson of Middleton, Barlow offered to buy Jackson's entire stock for its weight in gold. There was also the matter of beer bottles. Since many tulip shows took place in pubs, it was, and is, customary to display them for show in beer bottles, which provide excellent support for the stems and flowers. Sam Barlow, to raise the tone a little, designed a tulip vase made of black glass, not unlike the Turkish *laledan*, for use at shows – especially those of the National Tulip Society, which was founded in 1849.

The world of the florists was no Eden. Early in the nineteenth century they were much affected by the Napoleonic Wars, as Thornton had bitterly pointed out when *The Temple of Flora* had failed to prosper ('the once moderately rich very justly now complain that they are exhausted through taxes laid on them to pay armed men'); and James

'Sam Barlow', a florists' tulip from the Wakefield and North of England Tulip Society.

'Lord Stanley', a florists' tulip from the Wakefield and North of England
Tulip Society.

Maddock the Younger, heir to hundreds of tulips bred in his father's
nursery in Walworth, tried vainly to resurrect interest by getting
James Sowerby to portray them in *The Florists' Delight*. When peace
finally came in 1815, there were years of agricultural unrest, but nevertheless Thomas Hogg, a florist from Paddington Green, believed 'a
fresh spirit has been infused into the cultivation of tulips since our
return to peace',[12] and Mr Clarke, an experienced florist of Croydon,
led the field, appropriately naming his finest tulip 'Trafalgar'. But all
too soon tensions arose among the florists themselves. At first it was
about catalogue prices; as Thomas Hogg wrote, 'a modest collection
of choice tulips could not be purchased for much less than a thousand
pounds', and this was in the world of the nurserymen, so small wonder that the industrial north and Midlands took to rearing their own
tulips. As competition grew, the favoured types of tulips diverged,
the northerners delighting in colour and markings, the southerners

William Morris 'Medway' fabric design; this is the only Morris tulip design based on a florists' tulip.

insisting on form. A typical outburst appeared in the *Cottage Gardener* in June 1851:

> The Great Northern Tulip Show went off much to the satis-
> faction of the Great Northern growers and was especially

pleasing to those who cannot throw away foul tulips . . . They would not disqualify smudged-bottomed sorts, and the tulips which had prizes were a disgrace to the fancy.[13]

In 1847 Dr Hardy weighed in with an essay 'On Perfection of Form in the Tulip' in the *Midland Florist*, offering a host of geometric calculations and urging judges to take the measurements thus: 'the perfect curve in a tulip petal should be equal in radius to half the diameter of the flower.'[14] His strictures became known as the Hardy protocol and possibly helped distract attention from the north–south divide. Another sore point was the appearance of nurserymen and dealers advertising their tulips by entering the shows and upsetting amateurs. Among the amateurs themselves there were accusations of skulduggery, and sometimes the judges went in fear of reprisals.

When emotions and prices ran high it was, of course, a heyday for tulips. In 1854, 100 guineas was paid for a tall rose tulip, beautifully feathered, called 'Duchess of Cambridge', and during the 1860s some of the finest florists' tulips were still being produced, but from then on florists' societies declined in membership. Football clubs proved a rival attraction (in 1871 Association Football held its first cup final), and the urban sprawl of towns and factories, to which idealists like William Morris so objected, absorbed many of the original allotments. As the century drew to a close the florists themselves were dying off, taking much of their expertise with them. The nurseryman Peter Barr came to the rescue, buying up stocks of old tulips and launching them in his catalogue of 1893 with much publicity in the gardening press. Also in 1893 a lovely description of the Wakefield show appeared in the *Journal of Horticulture and Cottage Gardener*:

the exhibitors sitting around the table, every interesting point and detail in connection with the flowers are freely discussed . . . so much friendly rivalry and enjoyment derived from the fact that the beauty and good points of a flower are more to them than the actual money value of the prizes.[15]

'Habit De Noce', a florists' tulip from the Wakefield and North of England Tulip Society.

But by this time vigorous new hybrids of bedding tulips were being mass-produced by commercial breeders, especially in the Netherlands. Florists' societies became fewer and fewer until in 1936 the National Tulip Society had just two members, Peter Barr and Daniel Hall, author of *The Book of the Tulip* (1929). They subsumed themselves into the Wakefield and North of England Tulip Society, which still thrives, producing breeders, flames and feathers with old names like 'Habit de Noces' and 'Lord Frederick Cavendish' and new names like 'Akers Flame' and 'Wakefield' – 'sister seedlings, light crimson on a pure white base'.[16] Their show is held every May, and the tulips are displayed in beer bottles, as of yore.

Sir A. Daniel Hall was the person who, through his wide-ranging expertise, linked tulip breeding and modern scientific botany. He was responsible during the 1920s for breeding several tulips still grown by the Wakefield and North of England Society: the *bybloemen* 'Columbine'; the rose tulip 'Gleam'; and 'Cyrano', produced by crossing 'Sam Barlow' and 'Sir Joseph Paxton' and described as 'almost black breaks and rich plum shades on a golden base'.[17] As well as *The Book of the Tulip* of 1929, he also wrote *The Genus Tulipa* in 1940. Hall was prominent in practical horticultural and genetic research, becoming director first of the Rothamstead Experimental Station, and in 1927 of the John Innes Research Institute, the time and place when the cause of tulip breaking was finally discovered by Dorothy Cayley. She published the results of her experiments in the *Annals of Applied Biology* in 1928,[18] proving that tulip breaking was due to a virus infection, and describing how she had artificially produced the same effect by inserting minute amounts of tissue from a broken tulip into a normal bulb during dormancy. She concluded that the virus was transmitted by sap through the agency of insects and that the degree of breaking was proportional to the amount of infected tissue introduced. In the 1930s it was proved that aphids (greenfly) were the insect responsible, and viral strains were identified, ranging from severe tulip breaking virus (STBV) to mild (MTBV); there was also top tulip breaking virus (TTBV) and Rembrandt tulip breaking virus (ReTBV). These viruses, collectively known as TBV, belong to the group known as mosaic viruses, and the most prevalent also affects

Historic tulips in the Walled Garden at Keukenhof Gardens, the Netherlands.

peach trees. They (several viruses may be present in one tulip) affect the anthocyanin levels in the flower, which are responsible for the pink, red and purple pigments, leaving the underlying colour of the tulip petals, which is always white or yellow, to show through. Light-breaking causes the white or yellow to become exposed and the darker red/pink/purple tones to form streaks, spots, flames or feathers. Dark-breaking causes the darker pigments to be formed in excess, intensifying the colours in an exciting way. Average breaking means both types of breaking have occurred, with light-breaking in the lower petals and dark-breaking in the upper petals.

Thus the phenomenon which had mystified and enchanted tulip growers since the time of Clusius was finally exposed. Being a disease, breaking normally weakens the tulip, but not always fatally, and in the case of the surviving florists' tulips its effects are stabilized. However, virus is anathema to commercial growers; a diseased tulip in the bulb fields is always eliminated, and it is illegal knowingly to advertise and sell diseased stock. The streaked tulips known as Rembrandts were derived from the florists' tulips early in the twentieth century, and they were marketed until regulations against TBV were introduced. Any so-called Rembrandts now offered for sale, and displaying the streaked effect, must be achieved legally through cross-breeding, and not viral infection.

eight
Plant Hunters and Nurserymen
🙌

During the nineteenth century, while the fortunes of florists' tulips were waxing and waning, species tulips came back into the limelight with an upsurge of discoveries and rediscoveries both by professional botanists and interested amateurs. Henry John Elwes, for instance, whose descendants still maintain the legendary plant collections at Colesbourne in Gloucestershire, was an ardent traveller and member of the hunting, shooting and fishing brigade, who also had the sensitivity and skills of a plant hunter. In the *Gardeners' Chronicle* for July 1882, he described finding *T. primulina* (a pale relative of *T. sylvestris*) in the mountains of Algeria:

> This very pretty little tulip was found by me in the Aures mountains in May. It grows on the ridges and open glades in the cedar forest, though not very plentiful. It is extremely sweet scented. I previously knew of the existence of such a plant from a drawing and specimen collected by Mr Hammond at El Kantara, about thirty miles farther in the interior and beyond the range of cedars. It was the only good bulbous plant I found in the Aures mountains.[1]

It was characteristic of Elwes to generously give credit for an earlier discovery. He had done the same in January 1876 when *The Garden* described the red-flowered *T. eichleri* as 'a very showy species introduced by Mr Elwes'. The following week he replied: 'I do believe

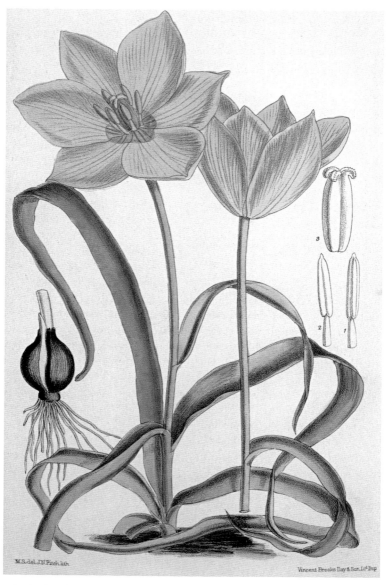

Tulipa batalinii from *Curtis's Botanical Magazine* (1904), named after Dr Batalin, a director
of the Botanic Garden of St Petersburg.

I was the first to flower it in England, but my bulbs came from Dr Regel in St Petersburg and my friend Herr Leichtlin of Carlsruhe.'[2] It was all a matter of networks.

Henry Elwes had been introduced to Max Leichtlin – perhaps by Joseph Hooker, director of Kew – in the mid-1870s, after Leichtlin had left the family business in Karlsruhe to set up his own botanic garden in Baden-Baden, a spa much favoured by Russian aristocrats and authors. In his youth Leichtlin had trained in the van Houtte nurseries in Ghent, which gave him expertise, but his modus operandi was more reminiscent of Clusius, since he became a centre of communication and plant exchanges (which he referred to as sendings) between private gardeners, plant hunters, nursery owners, botanic gardens, customs men and missionaries. One of his keenest correspondents was Ellen Wilmott. As a customer, Leichtlin indulged her desire to outsmart the commercial nurseries at horticultural shows (she placed prodigious orders with him), and as a fellow plantsman, he confided to her that he might pass a plant five or six times a day to watch its development and admire its colours.[3]

When a new tulip appeared on the scene, there was some confusion about where credit was due – whether to the plant hunter, the patron of the expedition, the botanist who named the flower (or the one whose name it bore) or the gardener who first brought it to flower on European soil. Max Leichtlin propagated and supervised the entry of many plants into European gardens, and he would write 'introduced by me' in his notes. *T. leichtlinii* was named after him (but it is now regarded as a variation of *T. clusiana*); *T. violacea* was credited to him (but it is now subsumed in *T. pulchella*); the introduction of *T. sintenisii* (a red tulip synonymous with *T. aleppensis*) was also credited to Leichtlin, although it was named after Paul Sintenis, the Austrian plant hunter who discovered it in northeast Turkey near Erzurum and sent it to Leichtlin. Paul Sintenis mostly worked as a collector for the great Dutch nursery Van Tubergen, founded in 1869. But of all the tulips Max Leichtlin received at Baden-Baden and coaxed into multiplying, *T. batalinii* (named after Dr Batalin, director of the Botanic

Garden at St Petersburg) most roused his patient determination. It is an ethereal, creamy yellow tulip of the Clusiana group, found in Central Asia and closely related to the scarlet *T. linifolia*. For years Leichtlin propagated *T. batalinii* in various shades of yellow, until a soft crimson variety emerged and two 'most rare' bulbs were advertised in *The Garden* in 1904. Meanwhile the Van Tubergen nursery had received *T. batalinii* from their collector Paul Graeber, on an expedition to Bokhara in Uzbekistan, and proceeded to produce cultivars (some of them hybrids with *T. linifolia* and *T. maximoviczii*), which now include 'Yellow Jewel', 'Apricot Jewel', 'Bronze Charm', the more orange 'Bright Gem' and the scarlet 'Red Gem'.

T. batalinii and a host of other tulips were botanically described and given their names by Eduard Regel, a German botanist and founder of the botanic journal *Gartenflora*. Regel moved to St Petersburg in 1855 and succeeded Batalin as director of the Botanic Garden from 1875 until his death in 1892. Regel was a keen taxonomist and, being strategically placed in Russia, he commanded the heights of tulip collection and classification while the Russian steppes were explored during the nineteenth century, and plant hunters followed in the wake of military and geographic expeditions across Asia. In addition, Regel's son Albert, who trained as a doctor, led the field as an explorer-botanist. He was appointed district physician in remote regions east of the Tien Shan mountains, and from 1877 to 1885 he conducted expeditions on behalf of the Russian Geographic Society, which were also recorded in the proceedings of the Royal Geographical Society in London with such accolades as 'Dr Regel to whom we are indebted for describing regions hitherto left blank in our maps'.

Albert Regel was the first to discover *T. praestans* on the steep slopes of the southern Pamir-Alai mountains; this species was distinguished by bearing not one but several large red flowers with pointed petals – although Albert Regel's variety seldom bore more than two flowers while subsequent discoveries achieved up to five, even seven. In 1903 it was given the name *T. praestans* (meaning 'excellent') by John Hoog, head of the Van Tubergen nursery, and in 1913

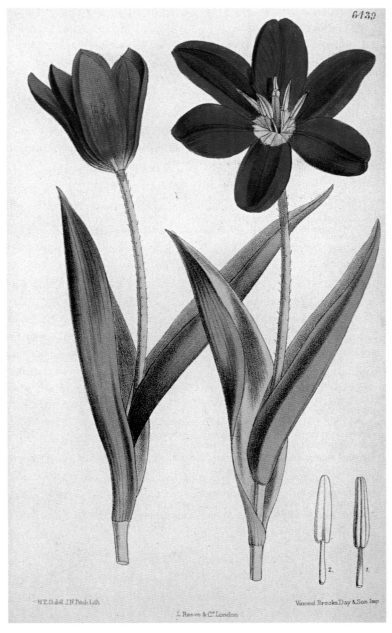

Tulipa albertii from *Curtis's Botanical Magazine* (1879), named after Albert Regel, plant hunter and son of Eduard Regel.

'Van Tubergen's Variety' was put on sale, with larger scarlet flowers and red filaments which 'came from a more northerly district than those collected in Bokhara and are early flowering'.[4] Albert Regel also sent his father *T. lanata* from the Pamir-Alai, and he named it after the woolly lining of its bulb tunic, although it had long been known and distributed in the Islamic East, where its red flowers adorned the roofs of mosques. On the other hand, *T. lanata* did not become commercially available in Europe until George Egger, another collector for Van Tubergen, who lived in Tabriz, sent John Hoog 'from 1929–33 a good quantity of the magnificent *T. lanata*'.[5]

Until his death in 1882 General von Kaufmann, governor of Russian Turkestan, often accompanied Albert Regel on his plant-hunting expeditions, and one of their most important discoveries, named after the general by Eduard Regel in 1877, was *T. kaufmanniana*, found in the western Tien Shan mountains in modern Uzbekistan. Known as the water lily tulip, its usual wild form is white, cream or yellow with a golden blotch. The flower is very dainty, though large, and its outer petals may be backed with red, purple or green, giving the potential for much colour variation. *T. kaufmanniana*, along with *T. greigii* (named by Regel in 1871 after General Greig, president of the Russian Horticultural Association), were the two most commercially important of Albert Regel's discoveries. *T. greigii* also grows in the Tien Shan, sometimes alongside *T. kaufmanniana*. It is easily distinguished by the purple stripes and splashes on its leaves, and its best-known cultivar, 'Red Riding Hood', has made this feature popular. The flowers are usually red, though even in the wild this plant is capable of producing yellow, cream and bicoloured flowers. Once again it was Van Tubergen's John Hoog who seized the initiative. Discovering that Paul Graeber, a German plant hunter living in Tashkent, had been sending quantities of *T. greigii* onto the European market via 'a horticultural establishment in Riga', Hoog sought out this 'man so fully equipped to collect bulbs in the steppes, who might also be useful to bring into cultivation the numerous tulips described by Albert Regel'. The deal was made that, 'for a given sum, Graeber

Tulipa kaufmanniana, the water lily tulip, growing in the Royal Botanic Gardens, Kew; named after General von Kaufmann, Governor of Russian Turkestan.

would travel up to the eastern frontier of Turkestan and collect for Van Tubergen. At the same time, others of Graeber's men, assisted by his wife, continued to collect *T. greigii.*[6] In fact, Graeber established a fruit garden and nursery in Tashkent and pioneered the far more satisfactory alternative of propagating bulbs in the nursery to sell on, rather than always digging them up in the wild.

Another of John Hoog's most useful contacts was Joseph Haberhauer, who ran a hotel in Samarkand and noticed that the peasant women in the market were selling tulips dug up in the hills that were larger and more brilliantly coloured than any he had ever seen. (This ancient market trade was probably the origin of all garden tulips.) John Hoog described Haberhauer as 'the man to whom we owe the magnificent tulip *T. fosteriana*' (named by John Hoog to honour Sir Michael Foster, professor of physiology at Cambridge and a member of the Royal Society). Hoog wrote:

> Haberhauer collected these in 1904 in the mountains near Samarkand and van Tubergen twice received important quantities. It is curious that the splendid variety which I called Red Emperor only appeared in the first importation, not afterwards. In 1914 Haberhauer penetrated deep into Bokhara and collected a large quantity of exquisite things. Alas the cases containing these arrived at the Russo-Austrian frontier as war broke out and were lost.[7]

These three showy tulips, *kaufmanniana, greigii* and *fosteriana*, have produced many commercial cultivars and hybrids, while each retains a recognized group of its own, which is defined by dominant characteristics. The Kaufmanniana group flowers early and is short-stemmed with funnel-shaped flowers of long, upright petals which open out into a star. Their colours range from the creamy 'Ancilla' and 'Concerto' to the orange 'Early Harvest' and the red 'Show Winner'. The Greigii group flower in mid-spring and is also short-stemmed; the flowers retain their original shape where the three inner petals are more upright while the three outer petals curve back; they are also more rounded than *kaufmanniana* petals; the leaves are mottled with purple dashes (although sometimes *kaufmanniana* hybrids have a touch of this). The best-known cultivar is 'Red Riding Hood', and 'Ali Baba' is also red; 'Sweet Lady' is strong pink, 'Cape Cod' is orange and there are also bicoloured forms such as 'Little Girl', which is pinky orange and cream. The Fosteriana group is taller and later-flowering, though still in mid-spring. The dominant colour is red, as represented by 'Red Emperor' and 'Mme Lefeber', which were originally the same stock.

A white *fosteriana* was named 'White Purissima', and from these arose the bicoloured 'Flaming Purissima' and 'Candy Floss'.

Perhaps Eduard and Albert Regel would be relieved that their own names are not associated with such developments. Their name-sake tulips are still wildlings with eccentric characteristics. *T. regelii* grows on stony mountain slopes in the Lake Balkhash area of Kazakhstan,

Tulipa regelli, from the alpine collection in the Royal Botanic Gardens, Kew; named after Eduard Regel, Director of the Botanic Garden of St Petersburg and himself a leader of tulip nomenclature.

where it survives extremes of heat and cold. Its broad, blue-grey leaves have several wrinkled ridges that run like crests from base to tip, a feature unlike any other tulip, although its dainty flowers resemble the Biflora group. *T. albertii* grows in the Tien Shan; Albert Regel found it near Tashkent, and it is capable of varying through many colours from wine-red or pinky orange to yellow. The flowers have a rhomboid shape, because the pointed petals bend inwards from a wider base, and its leathery bulb tunic is lined with dense bristles. It belongs to the group of tulips named the Eichleres, after *T. eichleri*, and its other relatives include *T. lanata*, *T. praestans*, *T. kaufmanniana*, *T. greigii*, *T. fosteriana* and *T. tubergeniana* – the last named by John Hoog after the founding family of the Van Tubergen enterprise. Ironically *T. tubergeniana* was later described by Daniel Hall (author of *The Genus Tulipa*) as a 'bad doer', except 'when it does flower it is very brilliant with that shining gloss characteristic of the Central Asiatic tulips.'[8] John Hoog's namesake, *T. hoogiana*, also belongs to this group with the glossy red petals, and has a basal blotch so tall and looped that the inner flower is almost black, as are the filaments and anthers. It was found in Turkmenistan by the redoutable Paul Graeber, but although showy, it never reached commercial heights, since its petals are thin and rather floppy.

The intrepid tulip collectors associated with the Regels and Van Tubergen opened the treasure box of tulip species to a degree undreamed of by their predecessors. But one of their equally determined precursors in the Far East deserves a mention. Philipp Franz von Siebold was employed as a doctor in Indonesia by the Dutch East India Company when, in 1826, he was sent to Deshima, the only European trading post then permitted in Japan. From there Siebold joined an embassy to Tokyo but was imprisoned for a year, and then banished, after he was discovered in possession of maps of the interior. Even so, Siebold managed to dispatch important collections of Japanese plants from Deshima, among which was the edible tulip, *T. edulis*, native to China, Korea and Japan and known to the Dutch as *amana*, after its Japanese name. Siebold said they ate the bulbs toasted like chestnuts. *Amana* grows at low altitudes in river meadows; the pale, drooping flower is tiny and veined with grey, and immediately below the petals are thin, leaf-like bracts unlike any other tulip. The structure of the ovaries is also different and it is tetraploid. Some, including Daniel Hall, do not classify it as a tulip, but it is certainly a variation on the theme. In Japanese albums of flower paintings it appears looking exquisitely delicate alongside the calligraphic descriptions of its usefulness.

Amana is not the only edible tulip (indeed when the Dutch were reduced during the Second World War to eating what was left in their bulb fields, they proved that cultivated tulips are edible enough, though bitter). *T. borszczowii*, with its extraordinarily fibrous and shaggy bulb tunic, was another tulip eaten locally, but unfortunately its indigenous name was not adopted; instead Regel named it after the

Tulipa borszczowii, an edible tulip, photographed near Lake Kyzylkol in Kazakhstan.

botanist who gathered it in Turkmenistan in the 1860s. In the 1880s James Aitchison found it growing near Herat and described it thus:

> In early spring the plains between Chasma-salz and Tirphul are coloured with this species which varies from every shade of red to pure yellow, the base of the perianth always deep purple. The natives collect and eat the bulbs, which are rather nice in flavour.[9]

Aitchison was a military doctor as well as a botanist. He began his career in India, then in the 1880s worked with the Afghan Delimitation Commission, which afforded him wonderful opportunities to investigate wild tulips, including the remoter habitats of *T. humilis*: 'This small tulip very like an anemone was common everywhere especially where there had once been cultivation.'[10] Once again there is the hint that the spread of tulip species owed much to human agency long before records began, since *T. humilis* is found throughout the Middle East and its close relatives – including *T. pulchella*, *T. saxatilis* and *T. bakeri* – grow westwards as far as Crete. *T. humilis* was officially named by the Rev. William Herbert (one of a fine tradition of botanizing clergymen), who gardened near Harrogate and who received bulbs from Iran in 1838 which had been collected in the Elburz Mountains north of Tehran. The similar *T. saxatilis* was known to Clusius and seventeenth-century European botanists, but had to be reintroduced by Henry Elwes of Colesbourne from Crete in 1880. *T. pulchella* was first illustrated in *Curtis's Botanical Magazine* in 1877 and introduced to wider cultivation by Van Tubergen in 1932. *T. bakeri* was named by Daniel Hall after George Percival Baker, who collected it in Crete and first exhibited it at the Royal Horticultural Society (RHS) in 1895. Some believe *T. bakeri* should be subsumed in the very similar *T. saxatilis*, though strictly speaking it should be vice versa, since *T. bakeri* is diploid and *T. saxatilis* is triploid, the higher gene count being an indicator of hybridizing. However, *T. bakeri* retains its name commercially and is best represented by its cultivar 'Lilac Wonder'.

Cultivars of *T. humilis* were popularized by Van Tubergen after their own collector, A. Kronenberg, sent supplies from the mountains of Azerbaijan. They are mostly rosy purple with a yellow blotch and the outside petals are shaded greenish grey, but a tulip collector's passion can be such that the possession of the cultivar 'Eastern Star' simply increases desire for the subtle differences of 'Magenta Queen', 'Odalisque' and 'Persian Pearl'. A. Kronenberg was an Austrian botanist, mainly based in Syria but travelling as far as Bokhara, who also sent collections of *T. polychroma* of the Biflora group; *T. linifolia* of the Clusiana group; *T. eichleri*, one of the glossy red tulips; and the entirely new *T. urumiensis*, from the northern shores of Lake Urumiya, which John Hoog received in 1928 – a tiny, scented flower, buttercup yellow with dark-green backs to the outer petals. Ten years later, in 1938, *T. aitchisonii* was named after James Aitchison by Daniel Hall. Appropriately, it is native to Afghanistan, where he plant-hunted, as well as Kashmir. It is related to *T. clusiana*; indeed, some authorities say it is only a red variant of *T. clusiana* or *T. linifolia*.

Another tulip named by Daniel Hall after an ardent enthusiast is *T. whittallii* although this is also a species which should possibly be subsumed in an earlier discovery, *T. orphanidea* (named after Theodoros Orphanides, professor of Botany at the University of Athens, who found it in the Greek Peloponnese). Both tulips are coppery versions of *T. sylvestris*, but *T. whittallii* is larger and lovelier. Edward Whittall, who introduced it, was another character worth commemorating. He belonged to an English family who settled as traders in Izmir in 1809. Like Henry Elwes, to whom he sent *T. whittallii*, he first became interested in flowers on hunting trips, but gradually his garden was filled with rare plants and horticulture became his main business. He employed local villagers as collectors but, in a satisfying turnabout, he also got them to replant his surplus stock on the slopes of the mountains near Izmir, and by 1900 *T. whittallii* had naturalized in their thousands.

Alongside Regel and Hall, another name to conjure with in the annals of tulip taxonomy is Alexei Ivanovich Vvedensky, who published

Tulipa whittallii, named after the English plant hunter Edward Whittall, from *Curtis's Botanical Magazine* (1943).

the section on tulips in the *Flora of the* USSR in 1935, updated since but not displaced, because Russia dominated the heartlands of nineteenth- and twentieth-century tulip collecting. The tulip *T. vvedenskyi* is another of the glossy reds of Central Asia (the Eichleri group), though capable of colour variation; the wide tops of the petals are triangular with a little twist that gives them a fluttering look, and the edges of the leaves are also undulating. The best-known cultivars are 'Tangerine Beauty' and 'Orange Sunset'. Vvedensky also took the rare step of naming a tulip species after a woman. This was *T. zenaidae* after Zenaida Botschantzeva, who had a distinguished career at the Botanic

Tulipa vvedenskyi, growing in the Alpine House, Royal Botanic gardens, Kew; named after A. I. Vvedensky, the eminent Russian botanist.

Garden of Tashkent and the Academy of Sciences of Uzbekistan and published an important monograph on the *Tulips of Central Asia* in 1982. *T. zenaidae* grows in the Tien Shan and is very close, if not synonymous with, *T. lehmanniana*. The flowers may be red, orange or yellow but are most attractive when the inner petals are yellow and the outer petals backed with red, giving a pattern of alternating red and yellow petals. Sometimes the yellow petals are feathered with red streaks, or have a raggedy edge, as if the gene that created the parrot tulip originally lurked in the Tien Shan mountains. In these remote valleys and slopes, new species, or variations of species, may still be found. In 2008 the lemon-yellow *T. lemmersii* was discovered by a Dutch expedition led by Wim Lemmers, a retired tulip grower from Lisse and a most experienced bulb hunter. *T. lemmersii* belongs in a group of species discovered during the twentieth century, related to *T. altaica* and *T. lehmanniana*, which is now subdivided into many more species with challenging names like *T. kolpakowskiana*.

Tulipa zenaidae, growing in Kashka Suu in the Merke valley, Kyrgyzstan; named after Zenaida Botschantzeva, botanist in Uzbekistan.

Camille Pissarro, *The Formal Beds by the Palm House at Kew*, 1892, oil on canvas.

The proliferation of names following the discovery of new (or slightly different) wild tulips ran parallel to the breeding of new garden tulips. Until the 1880s streaked tulips were far more highly valued, and plain-coloured breeders were grown only in the hope that they would break. Their mixed ancestry is not recorded, except for the 'Duc van Thol' race, known since the seventeenth century as Dukes, Ducs or Ducks. Their dominant ancestor is *T. schrenkii* (also known as *T. suaveolens*). They are single, early-flowering and low-growing, often distinguished by a clear, neat rim of contrasting colour round the edges of the petals, especially red with yellow margins. They appear sometimes in seventeenth-century flower paintings. The Haarlem nurseryman Nicolaus van Kampen praised them in his catalogue of 1739 as the earliest-flowering tulips, capable of forcing even in December, and the eighteenth-century London nurseryman James Maddock used them in his fashionable cut-flower trade. But it was when tulips were going out of fashion, in the second half of the nineteenth century, that the Dutch nurseryman E. H. Krelage bought up an important collection of Flemish florists' tulips in Lille, selecting the strongest breeders and renaming them Darwins (with the permission of Francis Darwin, son of Charles and great-grandson of Erasmus). They were launched in 1889, when Krelage displayed them outside the Exposition Universelle in Paris – where the Eiffel Tower also made its first appearance. The massed gaudy flowers caught the public's imagination, and millions of bedding displays were inaugurated. In May 1893 *The Garden* announced that the formal beds outside the Palm House at Kew were crammed with the new hybrid tulips 'giving colour to the elaborate arrangement . . . in a conspicuous position in the Royal Gardens'.

Inspired by Krelage's example, two English nurserymen, both called Peter Barr (father and son), bought up collections of English florists' tulips, selecting the breeders, and also propagated good doers preserved in traditional gardens, which became known as Cottage tulips. Some of the best were found in Irish gardens, descendants of the bulbs introduced by Huguenot settlers after the Battle of the Boyne. And on a trip to the Isle of Wight Peter Barr discovered purple/brown Treacle tulips flourishing in a little garden near Carisbrooke Castle. On the whole the newly introduced species tulips of Asia were not for the mass market, although some, especially *T. fosteriana*, provided important fresh genes in the twentieth century. Indeed it was all a matter of skilful hybridizing, patient selection and compensating for failures by the successes of commercial marketing. The Dutch always led the field, but the rivalry was good for business. In the end Peter Barr realized the Dutch tulips could not be outdone and instead he added them to his listings – most notably in 1907, introducing 'Sensation', bred in Holland, the first ever purple-and-white parrot tulip where all previous parrots were bizarres.

Tulips already had the largest share of the flower trade in America, and even before mass-bedding became fashionable in Europe it had been pioneered there. For instance, in the spring of 1845 six hundred tulips were planted in a New York public garden. In 1849 the Dutch nurseryman van der Schoot sent the first travelling bulb salesman to America, who visited the major East Coast cities and garden estates offering to undercut all rivals. The Philadelphia nurseryman

Henry Dreer, who represented E. H. Krelage, reported on his progress, but remained loyal to Krelage. American growers were never able to displace Dutch supremacy in tulip production; imports grew by hundreds of millions through the twentieth century, the terms of trade being balanced by the Dutch purchase of American flour – and when the Second World War broke out, and the European market plunged, Dutch tulips were exchanged for American firearms. From early in the twentieth century the new bedding tulips were also being supplied from Holland to growers across the continents wherever climate allowed, not only in Europe and Turkey but in the temperate zones of Chile, Australia, New Zealand, South Africa and even Japan (where the production of tulip bulbs fits in with the cycle of the rice harvest).

Visits to the Dutch bulb fields were a tourist attraction from Edwardian times, the patchwork strips of brilliant colours appealing to eyes adjusted to the aesthetics of bedding displays. However,

Claude Monet, *Tulip Fields at Sassenheim, near Leiden*, 1886, oil on canvas.

Charles Rennie Mackintosh textile design of stylized tulips, 1915–23.

some had their reservations about 'the bang in the eye which they give us', and turned instead to the new species tulips that Van Tubergen offered. The highly influential British garden designer William Robinson fiercely championed a more naturalistic style of planting, but Gertrude Jekyll, another exponent of traditional cottage gardening, maintained a painterly appreciation of the colour effects offered

Aerial view of bulbfields, the Netherlands.

by the new tulips. Although her most characteristic style relied on grey leaves and pastel shades, she also created dramatic highlights with clever contrasts, for which purple/black and crimson tulips were magnificent – or several tones of red, or yellow flaming through to orange. With tulips many effects are possible, from blocks of colour – exemplified above all by the extravaganzas of massed planting in the Keukenhof gardens in Holland – to varied interplanting with other spring flowers, which offers great scope for artistic and horticultural creativity. Timing is all, and garden tulips are still grouped according to the order of their flowering:[11]

1   SINGLE EARLY TULIPS, including the old 'Duc van Thol' race, with a cup-shaped flower on a short stem: for example, 'Orange Flair', 'Apricot Beauty', 'Candy Prince', 'Cape Town' (which is yellow feathered red) and white 'Diana'. They begin the tulip season in late March or early April.

2   DOUBLE EARLY TULIPS, also on a short stem, with an untidy mass of petals, flowering in April; including

Tulips growing in Monet's garden at Giverny. Normandy.

creamy 'Verona'; yellow 'Monte Carlo' and deep-pink 'Paul Rubens'. Daniel Hall, who felt double tulips were a mistake, called them 'sturdy little martinets with just that touch of the grotesque that appeals to lovers of the rococo'.[12]

3 TRIUMPHS are mid-season tulips, late April to May, taller and larger-flowered, with more colours and cultivars than any other group. They result from crossing the single earlies and Old Darwin tulips and include bicoloured flowers; for example, 'Gavota', deep-red with yellow edges; 'Shirley', white with pink/purple streaks; 'Arabian Mystery', purple with white

edges; 'Couleur Cardinal', plum-coloured with scarlet
edging; 'Princess Irene', orange with purple flames;
while some exciting single colours include 'Brown
Sugar' and 'Havran', which is nearly black.

4   THE DARWIN HYBRID GROUP, also mid-season, has
the tallest (bowl-shaped) flowers and the brightest
colours. Their genes include *T. fosteriana*, adding size and
the vigour to enable them to last several years (most
tulips need annual replacement). 'Red' and 'Yellow
Apeldoorn' are the classic survivors. The whites include
'Ivory Floradale' and 'White Clouds'; then 'Pink', 'Red'
or 'Apricot Impression'; while 'Olympic Flame' and
'American Dream' have striking red, yellow and orange
streaks.

Also in the mid- to late-season group are the tulips with particular
features including:

5   LILY-FLOWERED TULIPS with elongated, pointed petals
which are waisted like certain wild tulips, but much
larger. The group was formed in the mid-twentieth
century from Old Darwin tulips crossed with Cottage
tulips: including 'Merlot' 'like a glass of wine held to
the sun'; 'White Triumphator'; 'China Pink'; orange
'Ballerina'; and 'Aladdin', red edged with creamy white.

6   VIRIDIFLORA TULIPS, of various colours but with
a green flame always in the centre of their slightly
pointed petals. None is lovelier than 'Spring Green',
which is creamy white and green.

7   FRINGED TULIPS have petal margins like little pointed
teeth, mostly in shades of pink: these include 'Talitha',
'Louvre' and 'Fancy Frills'; 'Honeymoon' is white,
'Canasta' is red with white fringes, 'Cuban Night'
is dark maroon, and darker still is 'Black Jewel'.

Dora Carrington, *Tulips in a Staffordshire Jug*, early 20th century, oil on canvas.

8   PARROT TULIPS have petals that are extravagantly
    serrated, contorted and variegated; including 'Apricot
    Parrot', 'Blue Parrot' (mauve), 'Black Parrot' (deep
    maroon), 'Super Parrot' (white), 'Bright Parrot' (red
    and yellow), 'Parrot Lady' (cream and coral); also
    'Rococo', which is red, purple, yellow and green, and
    'Green Wave', which is pink and green. The season
    ends in late May with the late-flowering tulips.

9   SINGLE LATE TULIPS, bred from the Old Darwin
    and Cottage tulips. These cover the whole range of
    colours and have produced variations feathered and
    flamed with contrasting colours. They include 'Queen

Fringed tulips, one of the more curious forms produced
by modern tulip cultivation.

of Night', the most popular of the nearly blacks, and
'Black Swan'; 'Dordogne', orange with a rose-pink
flame; and 'Sorbet', which is white, and flamed pink.
10 DOUBLE LATE TULIPS are taller and neater than early
doubles or parrots, and are also known as peony-
flowered tulips: these include 'Orange Princess' and
'Red Princess' (sports of 'Princess Irene') and 'Uncle
Tom', which is maroon.

For most, this is what tulips signify – a bright harbinger of spring;
gaudy jewels in a garden or vase. Poets seldom like them – from the
time when Robert Browning in Italy saw 'the wild tulip like a thin,

Sir William Nicholson, *The Lowestoft Bowl*, 1911, oil on canvas.

clear bubble of blood', to Sylvia Plath in her hospital bed resisting
their vivid appeal: 'the tulips are too excitable, it is winter here.'[13] But
artists are far more susceptible to their creative invitations – it has
even been suggested that Mondrian arrived at his abstract blocks
of white, red, yellow and blue by growing up among the Dutch
bulbfields. The goblet forms of tulip flowers, whether rounded or
elongated, became an inspiration for Arts and Crafts designers, from
William Morris's floral patterns to the linear outlines of the Art
Nouveau and Art Deco movements, exemplified above all by Charles
Rennie Mackintosh. Meanwhile, painting vases of flowers with tulips
was released from the formula established by the Old Masters when
Duncan Grant (following in the footsteps of Cézanne and Matisse)
painted red parrot tulips against a swirl of textile patterns; and Dora
Carrington, placing her tulips in a Staffordshire vase that comple-
mented their lovely colours, breathed life into them by allowing them
to be asymmetrical and untidy. Cedric Morris planted and painted
the species tulips that he collected abroad to create the joyous, naturalistic masses of his flower beds at Benton End in Suffolk. Elizabeth
Blackadder, while capturing the way that tulips' petals shine, also

Gordon Cheung, *Tulipmania 8*, 2012, print with hand painting.

emphasized their fragile delicacy. But the final word belongs to Gordon Cheung, who brings the wheel full circle. His historic streaked tulips flaunt a harsh beauty against stock listings from the pages of the *Financial Times*. The artist himself is a reminder of what we owe to the East, and his tulips are a reminder of the thrill and danger of human desire, of which tulips have always, everywhere, been a symbol.

Timeline

龘

c. 1070	Seljuk Turks begin to conquer eastern Anatolia, creating the first ceramic tiles that feature tulips. The Persian poet Omar Khayyam (1048–1131) starts composing verses that make up his *Rubaíyat*, the first literature to mention tulips
c. 1180	The Persian poet Nizami (*c.* 1141–1209) writes the epic of Khosrow and Shirin; his poetry links tulips and love
1453	Mehmet II the Conqueror captures Constantinople and establishes gardens with tulips in his new city of Istanbul
1504	Babur (1483–1530), the first Mughal emperor of India, begins his conquests in Kabul, followed by the creation of gardens with tulips
1520–66	The reign of Suleyman the Magnificent, during which the use of tulip motifs in Turkish art reaches a peak
1553	Pierre Belon is the first European traveller in Turkey to describe tulips as 'red lilies'
1554	Osias Busbecq arrives in Turkey as Viennese ambassador and subsequently establishes a claim to have first introduced tulips into Europe and given them their name

1559	Conrad Gesner is the first European botanist to describe and illustrate a red tulip growing in in Augsburg
1560–70	The botanists Mattioli, Fuchs, Dodoens, Lobelius and Clusius all describe tulips in correspondence or publications
1597	John Gerard's *Herball* describes tulips growing in England and names James Garrett as their introducer, followed by John Parkinson's *Paradisi* (1629)
1601	Clusius publishes his major account of tulips in *Rariorum plantarum historia*, having first mentioned them in an appendix to *Rariorum aliquot stirpium* (1576)
1603	Roelandt Savery paints the first dated flower still-life with a tulip; Bosschaert the Elder's first dated flowerpiece is 1605, Jan Brueghel the Elder's 1606
1613	Basilius Besler publishes *Hortus Eystettensis*, the first German florilegium
1614	Crispin van de Passe publishes *Hortus floridus*, a glorified nurseryman's catalogue
1620	The fourth Mughal emperor, Jahangir, describes tulips in Kashmir, and his court painter Ustad Mansur paints one
1637	The climax of tulipomania, when the Dutch market crashes
1642	Adriaen van der Donck describes early Dutch settlers in New Amsterdam growing tulips
1650	Alexander Marshal is first recorded painting at Ham House in Surrey, after which his paintings of flowers are linked with John Tradescant the Younger, John Evelyn et al.
1650s	Jan Davidz. de Heem starts painting flower still-lifes
1654–74	Johann Walther paints *Horti Itzteinensis*, a German florilegium

1664	Nicolas Robert (1614–1685) is appointed court painter to Louis XIV, before which he had painted the florilegium of Gaston of Orleans, now in the Fitzwilliam Museum, Cambridge
1665	John Rea publishes *Flora, Ceres and Pomona*, listing several hundred tulips
1675–80	Maria Sybilla Merian publishes her *New Book of Flowers*
1682	Samuel Gilbert's *Florists' Vade Mecum* first uses the word 'florist' in a title (the first florists' feast was recorded in Norwich in 1631; the first London reference in 1677)
1688	William and Mary, the Dutch monarchs, come to the throne of England, Scotland and Ireland, bringing a fresh impetus to tulip fashions and gardening
1710	Joseph Addison and Richard Steele's tulip satire in the *Tatler* is published
1720s	Jan van Huysum (1682–1749) paints Baroque flower pieces
1726	Mehmed Efendi, author of *Lalezar i Ibrahim*, describes the peak of the fashion for Ottoman 'needle' tulips during the reign of Ahmed III (1703–30)
1730	The *Karlsruher Tulpenbuch* is published, it contains George Ehret's (1708–1770) early paintings of tulips
1735	Linnaeus (1707–1778) publishes *Systemae naturae* on plant classification by sexual parts, revised in 1758; and his *Species plantarum* in 1753
1761	Matthew Boulton endows the allotments in Birmingham, beginning a trend for workers' cultivation, which includes tulips
1789	Erasmus Darwin, after translating Linnaeus into English, popularizes him in *The Loves of the Plants*, a taxonomic poem

1799–1807	Robert Thornton publishes *The Temple of Flora*
1802–16	P. J. Redouté publishes *Les Liliacées*
1835	The Wakefield and North of England Tulip Society is founded
1840s	Massed tulip bedding is pioneered in American public gardens
1847	Dr Hardy, in the *Midland Florist*, establishes the rules for a perfect florists' tulip, known as the 'Hardy protocol'
1849	The National Tulip Society is founded, marking the heyday of florists' tulips, including the participation of workers like Tom Storer and industrialists like Sam Barlow
1854	Alexandre Dumas publishes *The Black Tulip*
1855	Eduard Regel moves to St Petersburg and becomes director of its Botanic Garden in 1875, leading the field in tulip collection and nomenclature through the expeditions of his son Albert and many others
1886	Claude Monet paints *The Tulip Fields of Sassenheim, near Leiden*; E. H. Krelage's Dutch nurseries introduce Darwin tulips
1889	The Paris Exposition Universelle features a massed display of bedding tulips by E. H. Krelage
1890s	John Hoog (1865–1950) of the Van Tubergen nursery in Holland leads the commercial collection and development of species tulips
1893	New hybrid tulips are described in the bedding displays outside the Palm House, Kew Gardens
1928	Dorothy Cayley publishes the first analysis of tulip breaking virus in the *Annals of Applied Biology*

1929	A. Daniel Hall publishes *The Book of the Tulip*, followed in 1940 by *The Genus Tulipa*
1935	Alexei Ivanovich Vvedensky publishes the section on tulips in *Flora of the* USSR
1999	Anna Pavord publishes *The Tulip*
2014	Gordon Cheung brings *Tulipmania* to contemporary art

References
🪽

1 Wild Tulips

1 Edward Schafer, *The Golden Peaches of Samarkand* (Berkeley and Los Angeles, CA, 1963), pp. 58 and 117.
2 A. I. Vvedensky, '*Tulipa*' [1935], in V. L. Komarov, ed., *Flora of the USSR*, vol. IV [Eng. edn 1968] (Leningrad, 1968), pp. 246–80.
3 John Parkinson, *Paradisi in sole, paradisus terrestris* (London, 1629), p. 52.
4 *Curtis's Botanical Magazine*, 839 (1805).
5 Anna Pavord, *The Tulip* (London, 1999), p. 312.
6 A. Daniel Hall, *The Genus Tulipa* (London, 1940); quoted in Pavord, *Tulip*, p. 312.
7 Pavord, *Tulip*, p. 314.
8 B. Gilliat-Smith, correspondence 1927, quoted in Pavord, *Tulip*, pp. 334–5.
9 Pavord, *Tulip*, p. 1.
10 Diana Everett, *The Genus Tulipa* (London, 2013), p. 4.
11 Richard Wilford, *Tulips: Species and Hybrids for the Gardener* (London, 2006), p. 12 (it is from Wilford, Everett and Pavord that this chapter's summary of tulip species has been compiled).

2 Turkish Tulips

1 *Babur-Nama* (*Memoirs of Babur*), trans. A. S. Beveridge (London, 1922), p. xx; and *Tuzuk-i-Jahangir* (Memoirs of Jahangir), trans. A. Rogers and H. Beveridge (London, 1978); also quoted in Anna Pavord, *The Tulip* (London, 1999), p. 38.
2 *Poems from the Divan of Hafiz*, trans. Gertrude Bell (London, 1897), p. xx, reissued as *The Hafiz Poems of Gertrude Bell* (London, 1995); also quoted in Wilfred Blunt, *Tulipomania* (London, 1950), p. 22. For the legend of Farhad see also Michiel Roding and Hans Theunissen, eds, *The Tulip: A Symbol of Two Nations* (Utrecht/Istanbul, 1993), p. 5.
3 Noel Malcolm, *Kosovo: A Short History* (London, 1998), p. 58.
4 *Poems from the Divan of Hafiz.*

5 *Rubaiyat of Omar Khayyam*, trans. Edward Fitzgerald (London, 1859–89), verse 43.

6 Philip Mansel, *Constantinople: City of the World's Desire* (London, 1995); quoted in Mike Dash, *Tulipomania* (London, 1999), p. 19.

7 P. H. Davies, ed., *Flora of Turkey and the East Aegean Islands* (Edinburgh, 1966–85), Chapter Two, note 7; and vol. x (1988), supplement 1.

8 J. M. Rogers and R. M. Ward, *Suleyman the Magnificent* (London, 1988), p. 166.

9 Ibid., p. 186.

10 Ibid., p. 85.

11 Pierre Belon, *Les Observations de plusieurs singularités et choses mémorables* (Paris, 1555), quoted in Pavord, *Tulip*, p. 35.

12 Philippe Fresne-Canaye, *Le Voyage du Levant*, trans. Henri Hauser (Ferrières, 1986), quoted in Nurhan Atasoy, *A Garden for the Sultan* (Istanbul, 2002), pp. 46 and 97.

13 George Sandys, *The Relation of a Journey Begun an. Dom. 1610* (London, 1615), quoted in Pavord, *Tulip*, p. 36.

14 *The Travels of Peter Mundy, 1608–28*, mss. British Museum, London and Bodleian Library, Oxford. See also R. Carnac, ed., *The Travels of Peter Mundy*, 4 vols (London, 1907–24). The comment on tulips is quoted in A. D. Hall, *The Book of the Tulip* (London, 1929), p. 37.

15 Robert Dankoff, *An Ottoman Traveller: The Travels of Evliya Celebi* (London, 2010), p. 21.

16 *The Diary of Dr Bennetti* (1680), quoted Pavord, *Tulip*, p. 45.

17 Seyh Mehmed, Mizami 'L-Ezhar, *The Manual of Flowers*, quoted in Roding and Theunissen, *Tulip*, p. 53.

18 The French ambassador, M. d'Andresel, was originally quoted in Le Père d'Ardène, *Traite des Tulipes* (Avignon, 1760), and in Blunt, *Tulipomania*, p. 27.

3 First Footings

1 Richard Wilford, *Tulips: Species and Hybrids for the Gardener* (London, 2006), p. 72.

2 Valerius Cordus, *Annotationes in Pedacii* (Strasbourg, 1561) and in facsimile as Conradi Gesneri, *Historia plantarum*, ed. H. Zoller and M. Steinmann (Zurich, 1987 and 1991); the tulip quotation is in Anna Pavord, *The Tulip* (London, 1999), p. 63.

3 Ibid. and quoted in Pavord, *Tulip*, p. 67.

4 Pier Andrea Mattioli, *Commentarii in sex libros Pedacii Dioscorides* (Venice, 1565) and Rembert Dodoens, *Florum et Coronarium* (Antwerp, 1568).

5 Matthias de L'Obel, *Plantarum seu stirpium historia* (Antwerp, 1576) and *Plantarum seu stirpium icones* (Antwerp, 1581).

6 Robert Browning, 'Up at a Villa – Down in a City', lines 23–5.

7 *I cinque libri di piante* (Venice, c. 1560), cited and illustrated in Ruth Duthie,

Florists' Flowers and Societies (Aylesbury, 1988), p. 67, and ill. p. 62.

8   Further examples are *The Lady and the Unicorn Tapestry, Sense of Hearing*,
    c. 1480, Musée Cluny, Paris; Anon. Flemish Master, *Virgin and Child
    Crowned by Angels, c.* 1490, Groeningemuseum, Bruges.

9   Nurhan Atasoy, *A Garden for the Sultan: Gardens and Flowers in Ottoman
    Culture* (Istanbul, 2002), p. 126.

10 Osias Busbecq, *Legationis turcicae epistolae quatuor 1554* (Antwerp, 1581),
    quoted in Mike Dash, *Tulipomania* (London, 1999), p. 35.

11 Pierre Belon, *Les Observations de plusieurs singularités et choses mémorables*
    (Paris, 1555), quoted in Pavord, *Tulip*, p. 58.

12 Florike Egmond, *The World of Carolus Clusius* (London, 2010), p. 19.

13 Ibid., p. 30.

14 *Mira calligraphiae monumenta* (Model Book of Calligraphy) (*c.* 1590),
    published as *Nature Illuminated* (London, 1997); the tulips appear
    on 23, 51 and 53ff.

15 Egmond, *World of Carolus Clusius*, p. 95.

16 Ibid., pp. 167–8.

17 Egmond, *World of Carolus Clusius*, p. 143.

18 Ibid., p. 178.

19 John Gerard, *The Herball or Generall History of Plants* (London, 1597),
    p. 146.

20 Ibid.

21 Richard Hakluyt, *A Brief Remembrance of Things to be Endeavoured at
    Constantinople* (London, 1581); quoted in Wilfrid Blunt, *Tulipomania*
    (London, 1950), p. 9.

22 Egmond, *World of Carolus Clusius*, p. 175.

23 Ibid., p. 112.

24 Basilius Besler, *Hortus Eystettensis* (Nuremberg, 1613); facsimile with
    commentary by K. W. Littger, G. Lorenz and A. Menghini, *Hortus
    Eystettensis* (Sansepulcro, 2006), pp. 99–105, plates 66–79.

4 Tulipomania

1   Florike Egmond, *The World of Carolus Clusius* (London, 2010), p. 171.

2   Simon Schama, *The Embarrassment of Riches* (London, 1991), p. 350.

3   Nicolaes van Wassenaer, *Historisch Verhael v–ix* (Amsterdam, 1624–5),
    quoted in Mike Dash, *Tulipomania* (London, 1999), p. 93.

4   Andrew Marvell, 'Upon Appleton House'.

5   Sam Segal, *Tulips Portrayed* (Lisse/Amsterdam, 1992), p. 17. For
    a survey of tulip books, see also Sam Segal, *Tulips by Anthony Claesz.*
    (Maastricht, 1987).

6   Anne Goldgar, *Tulipmania: Money, Honour and Knowledge in the Dutch
    Golden Age* (London, 2008), p. 10.

7   *Samenspraeken tusschen Waermondt ende Gaergoedt*; these Dutch pamphlets
    are quoted in all works on tulipmania, but most carefully analysed in
    Goldgar, *Tulipmania*, p. 173ff.

8 Mike Dash, *Tulipomania* (London, 1999), p. 146.
9 Ibid.
10 Goldgar, *Tulipmania*, p. 3.
11 Dash, *Tulipomania*, p. 168.
12 Goldgar, *Tulipmania*, p. 253.
13 William Brereton, *Travels in Holland, 1634–5* (London, 1844), quoted in Dash, *Tulipomania*, p. 223.
14 John Keast, *The Travels of Peter Mundy, 1597–1667* (Cornwall, 1984), p. 65 (excerpts from travels to Holland in 1639).
15 *Flora's Fools Cap*, scenes from 1637 engraved by Cornelis Danckerts after a painting by Pieter Nolpe, British Museum Department of Prints and Drawings; reproduced in Anna Pavord, *The Tulip* (London, 1999), p. 174.

5 The Artist's Tulip

1 John Rea, *Flora, Ceres and Pomona* (London, 1665), quoted in Anna Pavord, *The Tulip* (London, 1999), p. 119.
2 Paul Taylor, *Dutch Flower Painting, 1600–1720* (New Haven, CT, and London, 1995), p. 119; Taylor offers the most detailed background to this subject, together with Sam Segal, *Flowers and Nature: Netherlandish Flower Painting of Four Centuries* (Osaka, Tokyo and Sydney, 1990).
3 Cited in Taylor, *Dutch Flower Painting*, p. 116.
4 L. J. Bol, *The Bosschaert Dynasty* (Leigh-on-Sea, 1960), p. 33; Taylor, *Dutch Flower Painting*, pp. 126–8.
5 Taylor, *Dutch Flower Painting*, p. 130.
6 Rembrandt, portraits of Saskia as Flora: 1634, Hermitage, St Petersburg and 1635, National Gallery, London; *The Anatomy Lesson*, 1632, Mauritshuis, The Hague.
7 Taylor, *Dutch Flower Painting*, p. 98.
8 Paul Taylor, *Dutch Flower Painting, 1600–1750*, exhibition catalogue (London, 1996), p. 88.
9 Florike Egmond, *The World of Carolus Clusius* (London, 2010), p. 62.
10 John Parkinson, *Paradisi in sole, paradisus terrestris* (London, 1629), p. 45.
11 For further descriptions and images of tiles, tulipières and artefacts with tulip motifs, see Michiel Roding and Hans Theunissen, eds, *The Tulip: A Symbol of Two Nations* (Utrecht and Istanbul, 1993), pp. 25–49.

6 A Mirror of the Nations

1 Johann Jakob Walther, *Horti Itzteinensis* (1654–74), two albums in the Victoria and Albert Museum, London, and Bibliothèque Nationale, Paris; plates from the former published in Jenny de Gex, ed., *So Many Sweet Flowers: A Seventeenth-century Florilegium* (London, 1997), pp. 37–45.
2 Henry Peacham, *Book of Emblems* (London, 1612).
3 Robert Herrick, 'The Sadness of Things for Sapho's Sickness' (1648).

4 Alice Coates, *Flowers and Their Histories* (London, 1956), p. 251.
5 J. Caley, *Archaeologia X* (n.d.), quoted in Miles Hadfield, *A History of British Gardening* (London, 1969), p. 67.
6 Daniel Lyson, *Survey of London* (London, 1792), p. 522.
7 Thomas Hanmer, *Garden Book* [1659] (London, 1933), p. 21.
8 John Evelyn, *Elysium Britannicum* (London, undated), quoted in Prudence Leith-Ross, *The Florilegium of Alexander Marshall* (London, 2000), p. 96.
9 John Rea, *Flora, Ceres and Pomona* (London, 1665), quoted in Anna Pavord, *The Tulip* (London, 1999), p. 119.
10 Leith-Ross, *The Florilegium*, p. 150.
11 Sloane Herbarium, Natural History Museum ms. HS 131–42, see also Douglas Chambers, 'Storys of Plants', *Journal of the History of Collections*, IX/I (1997), p. 49.
12 Joseph Addison and Richard Steele, *Tatler*, 218 (1710), quoted in Wilfred Blunt, *Tulipomania* (London, 1950), p. 20.
13 Alexandre Dumas, *The Black Tulip* (1850), chapters Five and Six.
14 Charles de la Chesnée Monstereul, *Le Floriste français* (Caen, 1654), quoted in Mike Dash, *Tulipomania* (London, 1999), p. 32.
15 John Rea, *Flora, Ceres and Pomona* (London, 1665), p. 60.
16 Nicolas Robert, *Florilegium* (pre-1660), mss. Fitzwilliam Museum, Cambridge.

7 Botanists and Florists

1 Mrs Delany, diary October 1768, see Mark Laird and Alicia Weisberg-Roberts, *Mrs Delany and Her Circle* (New Haven, CT, 2009), p. 228.
2 Erasmus Darwin, *The Botanic Garden*, part II, *The Loves of the Plants* (London, 1789), p. 21.
3 John Sibthorpe and Ferdinand Bauer, *Flora Graeca* (London, 1806–40), vol. IV, 329f.
4 Pierre Joseph Redouté, *Les Liliacées* (Paris, 1802–16); partial facsimile, Peter and Frances Mallary, *A Redouté Treasury* (New York, 1986).
5 Robert Thornton, *Temple of Flora* (London, 1798–1807).
6 Samuel Gilbert, *Florists' Vade Mecum* (London, 1682), quoted in Ruth Duthie, *Florists' Flowers and Societies* (Aylesbury, 1988), p. 8.
7 George Harbin, *Memoirs of Gardening* (1716–23), mss. at Longleat; quoted in Anna Pavord, *The Tulip* (London, 1999), p. 130.
8 Philip Miller, 'Gardeners' and Florists' Dictionary' (London, 1724), quoted in Pavord, *Tulip*, p. 132.
9 Wakefield and North of England Tulip Society, *The English Florists' Tulip* (Wakefield, 1997), p. 8.
10 *Norwich Mercury* (11 July 1829), quoted in Pavord, *Tulip*, p. 218.
11 Details and descriptions in this section are taken from Wakefield and North of England Tulip Society, *The English Florists' Tulip*, pp. 30–35.

12 Thomas Hogg, *A Concise and Practical Treatise* (London, 1820), quoted in Pavord, *Tulip*, p. 218.

13 *Cottage Gardener* (June 1851), quoted in Wakefield and North of England Tulip Society, *The English Florists' Tulip*, p. 5.

14 G. W. Hardy, 'On Perfection of Form in the Tulip', *Midland Florist* (1847), p. 105; and 'Some of the Chief Properties of the Tulip', *Midland Florist* (1855), p. 135.

15 *Journal of Horticulture and Cottage Gardener* (June 1893), quoted in Wakefield and North of England Tulip Society, *The English Florists' Tulip*, p. 8.

16 *The English Florists' Tulip*.

17 Ibid.

18 Dorothy Cayley, 'Breaking in Tulips', *Annals of Applied Biology*, XV (1928), p. 529; and 'Breaking in Tulips II', *Annals of Applied Biology*, XIX (1932), p. 153.

8 Plant Hunters and Nurserymen

1 Henry Elwes, *Gardeners' Chronicle* (July 1882).

2 Henry Elwes, *The Garden* (January 1876).

3 Audrey Le Lievre, 'Max Leichtlin', *Hortus*, V (1988), p. 18.

4 John Hoog on *T. praestans*, *Gardeners' Chronicle*, ser. 3/33 (1903); p. 325.

5 Anna Pavord, *The Tulip* (London, 1999), p. 316.

6 John Hoog on *T. greigii*, quoted in Pavord, *Tulip*, p. 308.

7 John Hoog on *T. fosteriana*, *Gardeners' Chronicle*, ser. 3/39 (1906), p. 322.

8 A. Daniel Hall, *The Genus Tulipa* (London, 1940), quoted in Pavord, *Tulip*, p. 339.

9 Diana Everett, *The Genus Tulipa* (London, 2013), p. 187.

10 Pavord, *Tulip*, p. 312.

11 Richard Wilford, *The Plant Lover's Guide to Tulips* (London, 2015). This gives the latest classifications of garden tulips, with many illustrations.

12 A. Daniel Hall, *The Book of the Tulip* (London, 1929); quoted in Pavord, *Tulip*, p. 349.

13 Robert Browning, 'Up at a Villa – Down in a City'; Sylvia Plath, 'Tulips' (1961).

Bibliography

Atasoy, Nurhan, *A Garden for the Sultan: Gardens and Flowers in Ottoman Culture* (Istanbul, 2002)

Blunt, Wilfrid, *Tulipomania* (London, 1950)

Dash, Mike, *Tulipomania* (London, 1999)

Duthie, Ruth, *Florists' Flowers and Societies* (Aylesbury, 1988)

Egmond, Florike, *The World of Carolus Clusius* (London, 2010)

Everett, Diana, *The Genus Tulipa* (London, 2013)

Goes, Andre van der, *Tulipomanie: die tulipe in der kunst des 16 und 17 jahrhunderts* (Dresden, 2004)

Goldgar, Anne, *Tulipmania: Money, Honour and Knowledge in the Dutch Golden Age* (London, 2008)

Hall, A. D., *The Book of the Tulip* (London, 1929)

—, *The Genus Tulipa* (London, 1940)

Pavord, Anna, *The Tulip* (London, 1999)

Rogers, J. M., and Ward, R. M., *Suleyman the Magnificent* (London, 1988)

Roding, Michiel, and Theunissen, Hans, eds, *The Tulip: A Symbol of Two Nations* (Utrecht and Istanbul, 1993)

Schama, Simon, *The Embarrassment of Riches* (London, 1991)

Segal, Sam, *Tulips by Anthony Claesz.* (Maastricht, 1987)

—, *Flowers and Nature: Netherlandish Flower Painting of Four Centuries* (Osaka, Tokyo and Sydney, 1990)

—, *Tulips Portrayed* (Lisse and Amsterdam, 1992)

Taylor, Paul, *Dutch Flower Painting, 1600–1720* (New Haven, CT, and London, 1995)

—, *Dutch Flower Painting, 1600–1750* (London, 1996)

Wakefield and North of England Tulip Society, *The English Florists' Tulip* (Wakefield, 1997)

Wilford, Richard, *Tulips: Species and Hybrids for the Gardener* (London, 2006)

—, *The Plant Lover's Guide to Tulips* (London, 2015)

Associations and Websites

HORTUS BULBORUM, LIMMEN, NETHERLANDS
www.hortusbulborum.nl

KEUKENHOF, LISSE, NETHERLANDS
www.keukenhof.nl

PLANT HERITAGE NATIONAL COLLECTION OF TULIPS, CAMBRIDGE
UNIVERSITY BOTANIC GARDEN
www.botanic.cam.ac.uk

WAKEFIELD AND NORTH OF ENGLAND TULIP SOCIETY
www.tulipsociety.co.uk

Suppliers

AMERICAN MEADOWS FLOWER BULBS, USA
www.americanmeadows.com

AVON BULBS, SOMERSET
www.avonbulbs.co.uk

BLOMS BULBS, BEDFORDSHIRE
www.blomsbulbs.com

BRENT AND BECKYS BULBS, VIRGINIA, USA
www.brentandbeckysbulbs.com

BROADLEIGH BULBS, SOMERSET
www.broadleighbulbs.co.uk

BULBMEISTER, ARKANSAS, USA
www.bulbmeister.com

ODYSSEY BULBS, MICHIGAN, USA
www.odysseybulbs.com

A. FRYLINK & ZONEN, NETHERLANDS
www.royalpark.nl

Other

TULIP FESTIVALS IN THE USA
www.topeventsusa.com/top-tulip-events

ERIC BREED, LISSE, NETHERLANDS, TULIPS IN THE WILD PROJECT
www.tulipsinthewild.com

Acknowledgements

I wish to thank Diana Everett and Richard Wilford for their kindness and help in providing photos of species tulips, the former from remote habitats in Central Asia and the latter from the Alpine collections in the Royal Botanic Gardens, Kew. Both are the authors of recent works on species tulips, without which this book could not have attempted its task of simplification. A similar debt of gratitude is owed to Anna Pavord's great work, *The Tulip*. It has been like standing on the shoulders of giants. Thanks are also due to James Akers and the members of the Wakefield and North of England Tulip Society, who inspired my initial enthusiasm for tulips, and have given friendship, help and tulip bulbs over the years, culminating in the provision of some stunning images for this book including several from the archive of Maurice Evans. For research, the Herbarium Library at the RBG Kew was a mainstay, and the librarians always welcoming and helpful. Above all, thanks to my husband, without whose patience and technical help everything would have been far harder, and to our friend Chris Morley-Smith, who created the first draft of the map from a confusing list of tulip habitats.

Photo Acknowledgements

The author and the publishers wish to express their thanks to the below sources of illustrative material and/or permission to reproduce it.

Alamy: p. 119 (Peter Horree); Sebastian Ballard (cartographer): pp. 6–7; Pat Bishop: p. 169; © The Trustees of the British Museum, London: p. 49; Colourblends: p. 65 (Eric Breed); Diana Everett: pp. 10, 11, 15, 19, 20, 21, 27, 28, 177, 181, 186; Celia Fisher: pp. 23, 137, 192, 195; Courtesy Gordon Cheung and Alan Cristea Gallery, London: p. 197; National Portrait Gallery, London: p. 127; Shutterstock: p. 191 (R.A.R. de Bruijn Holding BV); Victoria and Albert Museum, London: pp. 121, 122, 146, 166; Wakefield and North of England Tulip Society/Maurice Evans Archive: pp. 159, 160, 162, 163, 164, 165, 168; Richard Wilford: pp. 13, 24, 73, 179, 185.

Index